DELIVERING ON
DIGITAL

The Innovators and Technologies
That Are Transforming Government

WILLIAM D. EGGERS

RosettaBooks®

NEW YORK   2016

RosettaBooks editions are available to the trade through Ingram
distribution services, ipage.ingramcontent.com or (844) 749-4857.
For special orders, catalogues, events, or other information, please
write to production@rosettabooks.com.

∞ This paper meets the requirements of ANSI/NISO
Z39.48-1992 (Permanence of Paper).

First edition published 2016 by RosettaBooks

Cover design by David Ter-Avanesyan / Ter33Design
Interior design by Corina Lupp and Jay McNair

Library of Congress Control Number: 2015949101
ISBN-13 (Hardcover): 978-0-7953-4751-1
ISBN-13 (EPUB): 978-0-7953-4757-3

www.RosettaBooks.com

To my wife, Morgann, the love of my life, who teaches me something new every day, and secondly to all the digital innovators inside and outside government who are giving everything they have to pull government into the digital age through a combination of vision, perseverance, and courage.

CONTENTS

Part III—Reimagining Government

Chapter 7

INTRODUCTION

After President Barack Obama signed the Patient Protection and Affordable Care Act into law on March 23, 2010, the administration spent the next two and a half years developing the "Obamacare" website. On October 1, 2013, with a final mouse click, the website launched. Its charter was unprecedented: to help millions of uninsured Americans painlessly sign up for health insurance.

It didn't work that way. On the first day, HealthCare.gov received 4.7 million visitors, but only six people successfully enrolled.[1] The website proved to be riddled with bugs and couldn't handle the traffic. After a month, a *total* of 26,794 people—only 5 percent of the administration's expectation—had enrolled in all the 36 states with a federal exchange.[2]

Some of the website's early issues were born of poor project management and bad planning. For instance, just a couple of weeks before the site launched, the administration decided to make users register on HealthCare.gov before they could shop around for health plans. This created a massive bottleneck in the website's registration system, as did the site's unnecessary insistence on identity controls for users who just wanted to browse. The eligibility system also mistakenly excluded multitudes of eligible individuals. So the $800 million website responded to both of its fundamental objectives—register new users and confirm eligibility for health care plans—with a resounding crash.[3]

The backlash was instant. Some called it a "catastrophic" failure; for others, it just added to a lengthy list of high-profile IT breakdowns. When President Obama apologized to the American people, he acknowledged the broader issue of the way the federal government develops IT: "There is a larger problem… and that is the way the federal government does procurement and does IT is just generally not very efficient."[4]

Ironically, though, the disastrous launch of HealthCare.gov might just be the best thing to ever happen to digital government in the United States. The public failure reprioritized digital government in a way that neither appointment, nor report, nor congressional testimony ever could: It forced the president, his top advisers, cabinet heads, and members of Congress to directly consider how a website should function, how digital services should be delivered—and to address fundamental problems with how government procures and operates IT systems. These problems remain deeply ingrained in the public sector's architecture. "Government has done technology and IT terribly over the last 30 years and fallen very much behind the private sector," President Obama remarked.[5]

It was the wake-up call of all wake-up calls. The shock to the system triggered a whole array of much-needed changes. The federal government quickly convened a new organization: the United States Digital Service (USDS), out of the White House— sort of a SWAT team to fix problematic digital projects before they ballooned out of control—and accelerated the launch of another, 18F, the government's digital studio in the General Services Administration, staffed by, as 18F put it, "doers, recruited from the most innovative corners of industry and the public sector, who are passionate about 'hacking' bureaucracy to drive efficiency, transparency, and savings for government agencies and the American people."[6]

Meanwhile, administrators untangled hiring rules to allow agencies more speed and discretion in tech staffing, part of an unprecedented recruiting drive to bring 500 of the tech industry's best and brightest into the federal government. (President Obama himself helped close the deal with some top recruits.)[7] Within a year, 18F and USDS had hired more than 120 techies with pedigrees from Facebook, Google, Amazon, and other tech giants. At the same time, the White House made IT procurement reform a top management priority.

With their extensive private sector backgrounds, this new generation of techies—whom *Fast Company* dubbed "Obama's Geeks"—contributed a whole different view of what technology is and how it can serve government and citizens.[8] With much of the public sector stuck in a mainframe mindset, this new group envisioned open-source tools and agile IT. While agencies historically defend their turf, this team aimed to help information flow freely across government agencies and programs. Most saliently, they introduced an unprecedented focus on the end user. Citizens who were once viewed as "customers" to be passively served as they stepped up to the window became active partners in designing more effective government.

DIGITAL TRANSFORMATION

An aging population, millennials assuming managerial positions, budget shortfalls, and ballooning entitlement spending all will significantly impact the way government delivers services in the coming decade, but no single factor will alter citizens' experience of government more than the pure power of digital technologies. Governments from Chicago to Seoul are in the midst of a historic (and frequently wrenching) transformation as they abandon analog operating models in favor of their digital counterparts. In 2012, President Obama summarized it like this:

> Today's amazing mix of cloud computing, ever-smarter mobile devices, and collaboration tools is changing the consumer landscape and bleeding into government as both an opportunity and a challenge. New expectations require the federal government to be ready to deliver and receive digital information and services anytime, anywhere, and on any device. It must do so safely, securely, and with fewer resources.[9]

In the broadest sense, digital transformation combines five modern technology components that are coalescing to change the way we work, shop, communicate, and travel.

- **Social.** Allowing people to communicate electronically in real time
- **Mobility.** Connecting with people wherever they are
- **Analytics.** Using data to do sophisticated analysis across programs and policy areas
- **Cloud computing.** Storing and processing information on a network of remote servers, which changes how you use technology and how you pay for it

- **Cybersecurity.** Providing secure communication and data storage

Tech-savvy organizations no longer view these five components as discrete solutions that address specific needs. Rather, they harness their *combined* power to target and build intimacy with customers and citizens at scale, and to better understand how and why clients, customers, and citizens buy products and services. For the most part, the business world gets it but the public sector lags behind.

To understand the power of digital transformation, look no further than your television. In the space of less than a decade, Netflix has gone from distributing DVDs by mail to online streaming to becoming a major content creator in the new age of television. For many, Netflix is the new TV.

And Netflix is hardly the only prominent example of digital disruption. In 2015, seven years after its launch, Airbnb became the largest hotel chain in the world—with more than 850,000 rooms and without owning any hotels. Uber, which owns no taxis, accounted for 55 percent of all shared rides in the United States—compared to 43 percent for taxis. That same year, Amazon.com became the world's biggest retailer.[10] Meanwhile, China-based Alibaba.com, the world's most valuable retailer, has no inventory.

These companies disrupted entire industries with novel business models that use digital technologies to fix a consumer problem, exploit a niche in the market, or both.

Digital is becoming the new normal. And digital technologies have quietly and quickly pervaded every facet of our daily lives, transforming how we eat, shop, work, play, and think.

And the transformation will only intensify as digital rapidly makes its way into the physical world. The continued evolution toward cheaper processors and faster networks has enabled a shift from desktop workstations to mobile phones and, now, to everyday objects, inspiring the term "Internet of Things" (IoT). Almost any device can be Internet-enabled, linking it to additional computing power and analytic capabilities that make it "smart." Think cars that can communicate with each other to avoid collisions, thermostats that can be controlled from thousands of miles away with a smartphone, and Internet-connected trash bins that communicate their status to help optimize collection routes.

The IoT represents both the next generation of digital technologies and also a new way of working. Kevin Ashton, who coined the term, describes this new way as one in which machines and other devices supplant humans as the primary means of collecting, processing, and interpreting information.[11] The exponential increase in data generated about everything and everyone presents governments with enormous opportunities—and huge challenges, since engineers need to build systems to analyze and derive meaning from all that data. That's where rapidly advancing cognitive technologies such as machine learning, artificial intelligence, and facial and speech recognition come into the picture. The increasing sophistication of these technologies can help governments to intelligently automate tasks, ingest and analyze massive data sets, and surface insights that augment human decision making.[12]

The bottom line: If there's one thing we know about technology, it's that it never rests. The thrust of this book is to help governments forsake analog, industrial-era models in favor of their digitally enabled counterparts. The goal is to help organizations orient themselves in the landscape of digital transformation and help set a plan for their journey. Importantly, getting from here to there is not just about the technology—it's a changed mindset that puts customers and users before organizational interests, turns human-centered design into an organization's core competency, and improves the way governments serve their citizens.

ESTONIA'S DIGITAL REVOLUTION

For a small, post-Communist country of 1.3 million, Estonia has a remarkable track record of firsts. It was the first European country to adopt a flat tax and the first country to enable online voting.

Indeed, Estonia might also be the world's most digitized government. Estonian citizens can access and use all kinds of local and central government services online in a matter of minutes. They can register a new company online and, in less time than it takes to finish a cup of coffee, start conducting business. Every citizen has a unique online identity, meaning he or she never has to fill out the same information twice when transacting with government, and citizens control their own data: They have access to a log where they can see every time a government official has accessed any of their data, and officials can go to jail if they don't have permission to view it.

It helps that Estonians are well versed in technology, with children beginning instruction in coding in kindergarten. Remarkably, Estonia's e-Residency program offers any citizen in the world— of any nationality—a government-issued digital identity and the opportunity to run a trusted company online.[13] It takes only five minutes to file Estonian taxes online because income information is automatically cc'd to the government ahead of time.

These big changes are just the beginning of the digital revolution that Estonia's government, led by president Toomas Hendrik Ilves, has delivered over the past decade. Ilves, raised and educated in the United States, learned to code in eighth grade—back before the rise of personal computers—and has been a technology enthusiast since. As ambassador to the United States in the 1990s, Ilves helped initiate a drive to computerize and connect all Estonian schools to the Internet. His reason for making "E-stonia" one of the most digitally advanced countries in the world is fascinating and worth quoting at length:

> The second motivation was reading a fairly Luddite neo-Marxist book by Jeremy Rifkin called *The End of Work*. The thesis of his book was basically that automation and computerization were going to be the death of work. As an example, he wrote about a steel mill in Kentucky that employed 12,000 people and produced X tons of steel. The mill was then automatized, and continued to produce the same amount of steel if not more with some 100 workers. From the Kentucky perspective, this was of course terrible. But from the Estonian perspective, it was intriguing, because our fundamental existential angst is tied to our smallness. So I reversed the logic and said that this was how we could increase our functional size by many orders of magnitude. In other words, if 100 people can do the work of 12,000, then my country does not have to suffer from the prevailing logic that economic success required an economy of scale. From there, I figured we ought to computerize as much as possible.[14]

It was because of this kind of vision that Ilves found himself in an enviable position when he hosted President Obama in

Tallinn in September 2014. The leader of 1.3 million people found himself providing advice on digital government to the leader of the country that birthed Silicon Valley. "I should have called the Estonians when we were setting up our health care website," said Obama at their joint press conference, only half joking.[15]

IMAGINING A NEW KIND OF GOVERNMENT

While Estonia sets the standard for digital transformation among central governments, plenty of cities, states, and provinces are pioneering digital innovations. Potholes, of all things, are a great symbol of the interface between what government does and what the public wants. Potholes are a government responsibility that directly impacts citizens (pretty literally) every day. In Panama City, the TV station Telemetro Reporta in collaboration with ad agency P4 Ogilvy & Mather agitated for the city to address its dreadful pothole problem by placing hockey puck-sized sensors in potholes that tweeted their location to public officials every time a car hit them.[16] Meanwhile, Boston's Street Bump app enlists citizens to monitor commutes with their smartphones and then uses accelerometer data to map pothole locations.[17] In a similar collaboration with citizens, Google has invented a sensor that maps potholes through sensors attached to each of a car's shock absorbers and then transmits this data so it can be used to analyze the road's condition.[18]

Of course some commuters prefer to let others deal with potholes, but even they can generate useful data. San Francisco's public transit system transitioned away from paper bus transfers to an RFID card, and the city's Municipal Transportation Agency can now assess average commute times, passenger density, and popular travel hours *by neighborhood* and adjust bus routes accordingly.

Ultimately, digital transformation means reimagining virtually every facet of what government does, from headquarters to the field, from health and human services to transportation and defense. The form and pace of the shift will differ depending on how public officials answer one central question: Is your service or program inherently physical, inherently digital, or somewhere in between? Much of what government does is information-based—and therefore inherently digital and convertible to bits and bytes. From taxes to unemployment insurance, from disbursing public assistance benefits to handling business license applications, governments process a massive amount of paperwork. In the digital age, the overwhelming majority of these tasks can be digitized end-to-end. In theory, this should result in huge cost savings and a far better—and more personalized—customer experience for citizens.

The state of Utah has digitized more than 1,100 of these basic processes, saving on average $13 per transaction or about $500 million a year.[19] Utah has even pushed paperless into services such as public assistance benefits, for which nearly 90 percent of recipients use the state's MyCase portal. Moving most of them to self-service, "no touch" approaches enabled the state to cut by 300 the number of FTEs devoted to processing forms. As low-touch and no-touch digital solutions continue to evolve, caseworkers can allot the time once spent processing transactions to the life-changing work that benefits families with complex needs.

Forward-thinking administrators can convert thousands of other activities to bits and bytes. Accounting and auditing, for example, have evolved from the days of manual journal entries to real-time detection of high-risk transactions, making them continuous rather than periodic processes. With most such labor-intensive activities automated, government auditors won't have to manually collect and check the data. Machine learning can scan, verify, and confirm transactions without any human intervention, leaving auditors free to perform more nuanced tasks such as fraud detection and risk assurance.[20]

A whole other set of government programs and activities are inherently physical: roads and bridges, schools and prisons, health care and child welfare, policing and building inspection. The list is long. Typically these brick-and-mortar activities represent some of government's biggest costs, especially at the state and local levels, and many of these activities will never be entirely or even mostly digital. Instead, they will become hybrid: part physical and part digital. The goal: Identify how the faster, more precise and more reliable information that digital technologies enable might contribute to better achieving the mission. Recognizing these opportunities typically requires government agencies to fundamentally rethink how they do business—identifying new models for service and adopting the technology and corresponding organizational structures to support them.

Take policing. Digital technologies such as mobile computing, analytics, and IoT applications can make physical policing smarter and less prone to error than previously possible. In Albuquerque, New Mexico, for example, officers use mobile devices to view live images and remotely control cameras mounted on mobile surveillance units that can be deployed to time-sensitive, critical situations such as negotiations with hostage takers or other SWAT emergencies. The system allows experienced officers to stay on top of events and provide instant guidance, regardless of their location.[21]

Sensors can also help the police by automatically detecting early indicators of an emergency or crime. Devices such as ShotSpotter can detect the sound of a gunshot and pinpoint its location to within 10 feet; by automatically alerting police dispatch, it obviates the need for a victim to report a crime and even detects crimes that might never have been reported.[22]

To address some of the criticism of overly aggressive police behavior, wearables, modeled on Fitbit and Apple Watch, could supplement body cameras by providing insight into police officers' behavior, enabling both real-time support and long-term coaching. Connected firearms offer the opportunity to track when a weapon is removed from its holster and when it is discharged. In the moment, pulling or firing the weapon can automatically dispatch additional support, while the accumulated record can inform coaching and development.

Similarly, monitoring stress levels, heart rate, or voice volume could make supervisors or fellow responders aware of elevated tension that might put an officer or the public at risk, allowing them to intervene immediately or debrief afterward on how to handle similar situations. This has particularly powerful implications in an era in which local police are increasingly tapped for crowd control or major-incident response.

Similar possibilities from digital transformation could influence everything from how education is delivered to how environmental quality is monitored. The key point is this: We will miss a huge opportunity if digital government just entails better versions of what currently exists (e.g., mobile access versus web access) instead of enabling changes at a much more fundamental level.

EGOV DÉJÀ VU?

These examples notwithstanding, readers with long memories can't be blamed for feeling a sense of déjà vu. After all, technology was supposed to transform government 15 years ago; an "era of electronic government" was poised to make government faster, smaller, digitized, and increasingly transparent. Many analysts (including yours truly, in a book called *Government 2.0*) predicted that by 2016 digital government would already long be a reality. In practice, the "eGov revolution" has been an exceedingly slow-moving one. Sure, technology has improved some processes, and scores of public services have moved online, but the public sector has hardly been transformed.

What initial eGov efforts managed was to construct pretty storefronts—in the form of websites—as the entrance to government systems stubbornly built for the industrial age. Few fundamental changes altered the structures, systems, and processes of government behind those websites. With such halfhearted implementation, the promise of cost savings from information technology failed to materialize, instead disappearing into the black hole of individual agency and division budgets. Government websites mirrored departments' short-term orientation rather than citizens' long-term needs. In short, government became wired—but not transformed.

So why did the reality of eGov fail to live up to the promise? For one thing, we weren't yet living in a digitized culture and economy—our homes, cars, and workplaces were still mostly analog—and the technology wasn't as far along as we thought; without the innovations of cloud computing and open-source software, for instance, the process of upgrading giant, decades-old legacy systems proved costly, time-consuming, and incredibly complex. And not surprisingly, most governments—and private firms, for that matter—lacked deep expertise in managing digital services. What we now call "agile development"—an iterative development model that allows for constant evolution through recurrent testing and evaluation—was not yet mainstreamed.

Finally, most governments explicitly decided to focus first on the Hollywood storefront and postpone the bigger and tougher issues of reengineering underlying processes and systems. When budgets nosedived—even before the recession—staying solvent and providing basic services took precedence over digital transformation. The result: Agencies automated some processes but failed to transform them; services were put online, but rarely were they focused logically and intelligently around the citizen.

Given this history, it's natural to be skeptical after years of hype about government's amazing digital future. But conditions on the ground (and in the cloud) are finally in place for change, and citizens are not only ready for digital government—many are demanding it. Digital-native millennials are now consumers of public services, and millions of them work in and around government; they won't tolerate balky and poorly designed systems, and they'll let the world know through social media. Gen Xers and baby boomers, too, have become far more savvy consumers of digital products and services.[23]

Meanwhile, public officials are becoming more tech-savvy, using every available medium to communicate to voters, constituents, and each other. And the incessant livetweeting, YouTube announcements, and Snapchat forays are intended to signal officials' literacy and competence in the digital environment. After all, the political stakes are higher than before: Every politician who watched the HealthCare.gov launch debacle is all too aware that doing digital poorly can go viral, sending poll numbers tumbling and political careers underwater.

Both user needs and provider capabilities have changed profoundly since the early days of e-government. Instead of desktops, most taxpayers now access government services with mobile devices; geolocation is everywhere, and the cost of sensors is plummeting, leading to their growing ubiquity.

Software advances are even more significant—not only the technological explosion you might expect but the entire process of developing and acquiring technology. Fifteen years ago, if you had an ambitious plan to digitize government services, you would have had to gin up a request for proposal, put the project out to bid, review proposals, and deal with—depending on the size of the contract award—inevitable recriminations and perhaps legal challenges. All this would take months or even years before you could tackle execution, with staffing and leadership from both the public and private sectors rolling in and out. When a solution finally materialized, it might or might not work as designed, requiring further investment of taxpayer dollars and personnel resources to fix and maintain.

Today, CIOs face a far less challenging IT environment on many fronts, for both public- and private-sector projects. Costs have plummeted because of cloud computing, improvements in commercial off-the-shelf software, and an explosion in open-source development. Software as a service—an approach in which software is licensed on a subscription basis and centrally hosted—means governments can have access to first-rate programs without having to build giant, expensive custom systems from scratch. And by breaking up large technology projects into smaller, manageable pieces, agencies can shrink the expensive, risky all-or-nothing projects that have characterized so many government IT initiatives over the past decade or two.

Not only has the technology changed—so too has the way digital projects are designed and delivered. For years, software development followed the waterfall approach, in which the process flows steadily downward, from requirements to design to implementation to testing, and finally ends at maintenance. The model has a major drawback: Changes after the initial deployment—and there are *always* changes—often prove to be cost-prohibitive, especially when teams must account for every detail and dollar in advance. To account for the fact that people rarely get a design right on the first try, developers shifted to an iterative model that allows for constant evolution through recurrent testing and evaluation, an approach called agile development. Most digital services in the private sector have abandoned waterfall in favor of agile approaches, and public-sector managers are beginning to follow suit.

In addition to agile development, a laser focus on the user and the rise of so-called "design thinking" and "human-centered design," which apply designers' methods to business issues, have propelled vast improvements in our collective understanding of how to build digital services.

This leads to another important difference between the e-government era and the current digital government: talent. All kinds of fields of specialized expertise that comprise the modern digital workforce—user experience and user interface designers, service architects, chief digital officers, and agile delivery "scrum masters"—didn't exist in any significant way in the dot-com era. Modern workplaces are filled with talented professionals who specialize in these and other digital-age occupations. And as we'll show shortly, savvy government agencies increasingly have a shot at getting their share of young talent.

More important even than the technical skills of this new cadre of technologists, however, is their entirely different mindset about how government work should be completed and what services should be provided. This shift in mindset, detailed in chapter 1, just might be the most critical factor for success this time around in the effort to digitally change government.

THE JOURNEY TO DIGITAL TRANSFORMATION

This book has two principal goals: to explain how governments can take advantage of the digital revolution to better deliver services, and to give innovators a set of tools to navigate the journey.

Truly changing government through the power of technology will indeed be a journey. In researching this book, we surveyed more than 1,200 government officials on digital transformation and interviewed another 200 government leaders. This research informs this book throughout, but one data point that is worth sharing now is that governments today are at very different stages in this journey. A small percentage might be considered "digitally maturing," but the overwhelming majority of them are still in the early or developing stages of digital transformation.[24]

Even for agencies ahead of the curve, the journey to digital government will be challenging. The good news is that today's digital innovators face more favorable conditions than their predecessors, and thanks to years of trial and error, we know far more about what it takes to succeed. This doesn't mean that the transition will be an easy one—or even that most initiatives will succeed. Very few things in government are easy, and cultural shifts such as digital transformation are hard to effect. Legacy systems, culture, procurement rules, missing workforce skill sets, limited funding, competing priorities, political leadership, cyber-security, and lack of an overall digital strategy constitute serious hurdles that leaders will have to overcome. Each of these will be addressed in more depth over the course of the book.

Here's a quick guide to how the book is organized.

Part I, "The Digital Way of Thinking," explores the vast differences between traditional government practice and the digital way of working and thinking. The digital mindset has five principal characteristics: open, user-focused, co-created, simple, and agile.

Part II is called "Hacking Bureaucracy." Most people think of hacking in a pejorative sense: breaking into computer systems and wreaking havoc on companies, governments, and often personal information. In the digital world, however, hacking also has a different meaning: to use ingenuity and digital prowess to fix a problem. "In the software development community, *hacker* describes the way someone thinks and works rather than a malicious activity—hackers are problem solvers," explains Greg Godbout, chief technology officer at the Environmental Protection Agency and co-founder of 18F. "We consider ourselves hackers in that positive sense: productively disruptive and curious."[25] In this spirit, the central argument in Part II is that most established government processes—hiring, training, project delivery, procurement, bureaucratic silos, security—are incompatible with a digital way of working and thus need to be reformed and redesigned (or hacked, in the best sense of the word) to achieve digital trans-formation. The good news: Digital innovators around the world are creating ways to reform and modernize these long-standing bureaucratic processes.

Part III, "Reimagining Government," challenges the reader to think about fundamentally reimagining government in the digital age—how the public sector can use digital technologies to rethink how they deliver services and achieve their mission. To this end, Part III explores the frontiers of digital government, going beyond efficiency and effectiveness to envisioning very different models for traditional public services, ranging from child welfare to the local Department of Motor Vehicles.

Chapter 1 will look at the change of mindset needed to deliver on the promise of digital technologies.

PART I

THE DIGITAL WAY OF THINKING

CHAPTER 1

THE DIGITAL MINDSET

"Hello, I'm Mike Bracken. I'm from the Internet." That's how the former chief digital officer for the United Kingdom opened his speech on civil service reform at the Institute for Government in London.

Over the next hour, Bracken, the co-founder of the UK's Government Digital Service (GDS) unit, launched a frontal assault on many of the traditions and beliefs that formed the foundation of Her Majesty's Civil Service.

The UK's venerated Whitehall model is predicated on the notion of a civil service driven by generalist policymakers trained to understand ambiguity, see an issue from all sides, and provide detailed policy options to ministers. Bracken believes instead in flooding government with digital innovators and letting them lead. "They're the ones who run successful organizations now, because they're the ones who know how to," he argues.

Traditionalists advocate the "interest and desire to get things right the first time."[1] Bracken pushes back arguing that, "It's much better to fail fast, fail cheap, and then put things right at a fraction of the cost."

The most coveted jobs in the civil service have long been the senior policy advisors who get to whisper into the ears of ministers. Bracken believes ministers should instead take their counsel from others. "Advice must come from the doers—the people at the coal face that understand the shortcomings of their services and who are brimming with ideas for how to make them better," he says.

And while Whitehall hails policy as paramount, Bracken wants *delivery*, not policy, to be the fundamental organizing principle of civil service.[2] He calls current policymaking slow, inflexible, unnecessarily complicated, adverse to technology, and afraid of change.

"The service should speak for itself, so policy can usually be articulated as one page of strategic outcomes that you're trying to achieve: get more people to use a benefit or less to use a benefit, something like that," Bracken says. "You don't need these sort of highly intellectual, flowery white papers behind them."[3]

Many senior British civil servants will—and did—strongly disagree with Bracken's pointed critique. One could argue about who's right or wrong. For our purposes, what matters is that Bracken, who has a superstar following among the digital cognoscenti, represents a radically different worldview, more akin to the Silicon Valley mindset than the typical attitudes of senior public officials. Let's call this worldview the digital mindset, one shared by a large cadre of new digital leaders in governments from Washington to London, from Tallinn to Seoul.

As governments embark on their digital journeys, it's important to recognize that "being digital" is about far more than technology—it's a changed mindset. Digital transformation requires seeing old problems and old processes through new eyes.

A digital mindset is simply different from the attitudes driving most organizations, especially in the public sector. It's a different way of thinking about customers; a different way of launching products and services; a different way of working.

Bracken exemplifies this mindset. He's a digital guy through and through. Before launching the UK's Government Digital Service effort, he led the digital transformation of the *Guardian* newspaper, and earlier co-founded an e-democracy site called My Society. He holds a firm set of beliefs about how technology can transform business, society and government, and has devoted his career to making his vision a reality.

"I've worked in five industries in 15 countries, and I've experienced the process of digital transformation many, many times," he says. "Digital is *the* technological enabler of this century. And, in any sector you care to name, it's been the lifeblood of organizations that have embraced it, and a death sentence for those that haven't."[4]

Bracken's sentiments are shared by many luminaries across the world, from presidents to princes. "New technologies, changing power relationships, failing jurisdictions, and disrupted economic sectors (i.e., the Uberization of everything) are challenging the status quo," says the Netherlands' Prince Constantijn van Oranje-Nassau, a senior advisor to the European Commission. "If government is not able to reform and apply new technology, I have very strong doubts that it will be able to effectively manage the challenges posed by pervasive technology developments."[5]

In Asia, more and more government leaders from Singapore to Vietnam to South Korea now hold the digital mindset. "Governments of the past used to work as 'vending machine–like' service purveyors, which offered the public standardized public services in a monopolistic manner," says Park Chan-woo, South Korea's deputy minister for the Ministry of Public Administration. "Now, governments are evolving into platform-like ones, on which the

PART II

HACKING BUREAUCRACY

CHAPTER 2

HACKING HIRING AND TRAINING:
Developing Digital Capacity

Suppose you could launch government digital services from scratch. How would you do it? Of course, for 99.99 percent of the public sector's workforce, this is purely hypothetical and completely removed from the reality of the 30-year-old IT systems that power so many government programs.

To the young team at the newly created Consumer Financial Protection Bureau (CFPB), however, this question was anything *but* hypothetical. In 2011, they had the opportunity to start from scratch in building a digital-age organization. And in Elizabeth Warren, a special adviser to the president who was instrumental in creating CFPB, they had a strong political champion to back their efforts.

Created by Congress and the Obama administration in response to the 2007 financial crisis, CFPB has a profound consumer focus. Its mission is to make markets for consumer financial products and services work better for consumers, whether they're choosing a credit card or applying for a mortgage.

With the opportunity for a digital-first approach, CFPB attracted to its ranks some of the best and brightest of the digital government community, doers who believed passionately in the power of digital technology to improve government.

Matthew Burton epitomized this new breed. He was part of a cadre of young millennial technologists who gravitated to Washington because they wanted to make a difference and were passionate about open data, open-source code, and open problem solving approaches. Before joining CFPB, Burton had spent five years helping the intelligence community adapt to using open-source and collaborative tools. "I started out as a thorn in the intelligence community's side because I was always complaining about how they undertook IT projects," he recalls. "Over time, my ideas got some recognition."

Burton, who became CFPB's deputy CIO, and the CFPB team adopted a few basic core principles for their digital approach: Start small, pursue open-source options when possible, recruit the best possible digital talent, and use digital tools to engage the public throughout.

"Just like a private organization, a government agency has to answer an existential question in its early days," Burton says. "If we want to succeed, we absolutely have to get X right. For the CFPB, technology was one of the answers.... At every level, from educating the public on personal finance to supervising banks, technology is seen as a driving force."[1]

Among other things, Burton realized early on that this meant his employees needed the best possible tools to do their jobs. CFPB developers can use open-source software, install modern code editors, and test their work with browsers such as Chrome and Firefox. He explains:

> If you decide it's time to start giving your citizen-customers professional-grade products, you can't do it without giving your staff professional-grade tools. Do not hire lots of designers and developers

and then force them to work with the same tools you provide your accountants and legal staff. They will fail, and you will waste money.[2]

CFPB explicitly set out to do things differently. But that isn't easy in government.

"We were told no to just about everything we wanted to do," says Merici Vinton, the agency's first digital lead.[3] Like Eric Mill, introduced in the previous chapter, Vinton cut her digital teeth at the Sunlight Foundation. "The Sunlight Foundation had a big influence on how a generation of us thought about government technology and transparency," she says.[4]

Vinton was recruited to the CFPB by Eugene Huang, its acting CTO at the time. Recounting their meeting over coffee, Vinton recalls the points she laid out when Huang asked her how she'd make digital technologies work in government:

1. Never build a website that's too big to fail; instead, start small.
2. Let's do open-source when possible (preferably always).
3. Let's build the capacity to do in-house strategy, design, and tech.[5]

And that's exactly what they did. CFPB assembled a formidable team of web designers and developers and made sure they worked together rather than in silos. It fostered innovation, which Burton defines as a culture of efficient problem solving. CFPB put its "curious, creative people into an environment full of interesting problems and gave them the freedom to pursue their ideas."

Today, CFPB works hard to maintain its culture of innovation. Every other Friday at the agency is "Dev Team Hootenanny," when web developers share updates on side projects and ideas—things to which they can devote 20 percent of their work hours. Victor Zapanta, the twentysomething web developer who designed CFPB's sleek website, calls this "nerd show-and-tell."[6]

Zapanta works with Audrey Chen, the bureau's creative director. Before joining CFPB, Chen was a senior designer at Comedy Central, better known for reengineering websites for *The Daily Show* and *The Colbert Report* than she was for government work.

"I'm excited by things that need fixing," Chen says. With a strong focus on user experience, she worked on some of the bureau's open and data-driven digital campaigns such as "Know Before You Owe" (to prevent homeowners and students from getting in over their heads in debt), and the Consumer Complaint Database, which publishes and analyzes complaints about financial products. "Democracy doesn't work if it's not usable—if you can't participate," Chen says.[7]

CFPB was the first federal agency to create its own digital design shop and recruit designers such as Chen. "Our whole culture was driven by design," Burton says. The whole technology team understood the importance of a great online experience. "We couldn't compare ourselves just to government websites," says Vinton. "We knew [we] had to live up to the *best* consumer websites."

So how did CFPB find curious and creative individuals such as Vinton, Zapanta, and Chen? Federal hiring guidelines are time-consuming and often wholly unsuited for a technology enterprise. Conventional criteria such as formal education and

STRATEGY DRIVES DIGITAL MATURITY

When Maude and Bracken launched the UK's "digital-by-default" framework, they began by developing a roadmap called *Government Digital Strategy*. In the US, the White House issued a similar directive, *Building a 21st Century Digital Government*. Around the world, we see similar examples of governments devising strategies for digital efforts.

This work is important. Our research points to a strong link between an organization's success and the presence of a digital strategy.

Governments with a clear, coherent digital strategy are better equipped to respond to opportunities and threats, and are more likely to foster innovation and collaboration. A digital strategy can be the determining factor for a host of aspects of the organization, from its willingness to take risks to its employees' level of confidence.

The US Department of the Treasury provides an example of a well-formed digital strategy. It created a detailed plan of action for each milestone mentioned in the White House's *Digital Government Strategy*, and a process to monitor and track progress. Treasury's strategy articulates some of the most important tenets: openness by default, consumer feedback, citizen engagement, and a governance structure designed to develop and deliver digital services to citizens. It also emphasizes the need to upgrade and adopt technologies and instill transparency both within and outside the department.

years of experience may not be nearly as relevant as demonstrable expertise with a particular software.

"If I need an expert in Git [an open-source version control software], I'm not *going* to find anyone with 15 years of experience, because Git—like most other modern web technologies—is less than 10 years old," Burton says. "In hiring web talent, we had to fit the square peg of digital culture through the federal government's round hole." Working with his HR department, Burton made initial application reviews less restrictive and broadened the minimum qualifications.

To draw the best talent, the CFPB recruited in the true sense of the word, hunting for specific skills where they could be found—at portals such as 37signals, Stack Overflow, and GitHub—rather than relying solely on USAJobs.gov.

The quest for top talent led to some truly creative recruiting. Techies love to snoop around website source codes, just as car enthusiasts like to see what's under the hood. CFPB placed ads for open positions inside the source code of its website. While this wasn't the first time an organization had done this, it's not exactly standard procedure for government.

Today, CFPB is built on open-source and known for its digital engagement with citizens. Beginning with a clean slate was a huge advantage, but CFPB offers lessons that could benefit any agency. As Vinton says, "Working in government can be awesome. It's up to the leadership in each agency to decide to make their organization a place where developers and designers want to work."[8]

And because digitally savvy leadership is so critical to digital transformation, we now consider the kind of leader it takes to drive such change.

DIGITAL LEADERSHIP

The question of who should lead an agency's digital transformation has two answers, because it requires two people: a political sponsor to champion the initiative and a hard-charging executive to drive it through the bureaucracy.

The sponsor's job is to champion digital transformation and provide political cover when it conflicts with traditional ways of working—as ambitious digital efforts almost always do.

Sir Francis Maude, who helped launch the UK's Government Digital Service (GDS), is a near-perfect model for the kind of political leader needed for digital projects. While in opposition, Maude developed the Tory's government reform program. He's a seasoned political veteran with more than three decades of experience inside and outside government (including the treasury, cabinet, and foreign office) and, critically, a trusted confidant and advisor to Prime Minister David Cameron.

After becoming head of the Cabinet Office in 2010, Maude launched the Efficiency and Reform Group (ERG) to drive down the cost of government. "Maude was a ruthless efficiency-seeker," recalls a senior official who worked with him when he was advising Cameron. "He was constantly saying 'This is wasteful. This is shameful, it's morally wrong and we need to fix it and drive it through.'"[9]

Maude followed up his efficiency drive with an equally ambitious effort to reform civil service in 2012.[10] His third major reform was to make "digital by default" the UK's tech strategy, with the aim of providing government services through fast, simple, and easy-to-use digital interfaces.

"These new digital and technology platforms are the foundations of our new civic infrastructure, a modern equivalent to

London's Victorian sewer network, or the building of the National Grid," says Maude.[11] As such, he envisioned a digital strategy built into policy, so it wouldn't be seen as a stand-alone reform plan (see page 44). He deliberately made digital service a part of overall civil service reform, with the goal of creating a civil service that was "less bureaucratic, skilled, digital, and unified."[12] "One key thing," Maude says, "is to get digital upstream as close to policy as possible. You need to empower people to push back against policy when it runs counter to a digital way of working."

Maude also realized that the UK government, which at the time had a huge debt burden, had to radically change to remain solvent. "We had the most burning of burning platforms," he says. "We had no money. We had to do things differently."[13]

A big part of Maude's effort was standing up to the status quo. GDS made countless decisions that upset other ministers, particularly when it denied IT projects it deemed wasteful or duplicative. Maude's fellow ministers would go to him to overturn the decisions, but by all accounts he stood firm, backing up GDS.

"For us, the epitome of political leadership was Francis Maude," says Kathy Settle, the former director for digital policy and departmental engagement at GDS. "Without his vision, his drive, his willingness on occasion to have fights with his ministerial colleagues to drive through decisions—without that, we would not have gotten as far as fast as we have."[14]

But politicians such as Maude have many responsibilities, so it's unrealistic to think they can personally drive each and every change through government. They need partners.

Maude found his partner in Mike Bracken, the technology specialist we met in the previous chapter. Calling it "the devil's own job," Bracken was asked to get nearly two dozen government departments moving the way Maude and GDS wanted. He talked about the challenge in a 2011 blog post, written the day he joined GDS:

> So I signed up. I've been watching this unfold for 15 years. We've had some success at *The Guardian* in the last few years, but this challenge is far greater: to improve the quality of digital public service provision for every person in the UK.[15]

Bracken's counterpart in the United States was Mikey Dickerson, brought in by US CTO Todd Park to help fix HealthCare.gov during its crisis. He remembers getting a call from Park, and looking him up on Wikipedia as they spoke. A few conversations later, Dickerson was on a plane to DC.

After salvaging HealthCare.gov—something Dickerson describes as more important and meaningful than anything he could have accomplished in a lifetime at his old job—he went back to Google. "I went back to my old job and tried to care about it," he says. "I was not successful."[16]

Dickerson soon came back into government to lead the US Digital Service. There, he and his team took the same methods they used to turn around HealthCare.gov and applied them to other projects. His appointment to the USDS got a lot of attention, and so did his casual style, his rumpled shirts providing a stark contrast to normal White House attire. "People want to know if I'm wearing a suit to work every day," he says, "because that's just the quickest shorthand way of asking: 'Is this just the same old business as usual, or are they actually going to listen?'"[17]

"One of the reasons Mikey has been so successful is that he has a seat at the table," says one observer. "He has a direct line to the president of the United States." This relationship gives Dickerson what he calls "hard power," allowing him to take on problems others can't. "Quite simply, the president can (and does) ask his cabinet secretaries to take seriously any USDS overtures to work on projects within their agencies," writes *Fast Company*'s Jon Gertner.[18]

Another smart move was nestling the USDS within the Office of Management and Budget. This "gives the techies muscle within various agencies and an ability to influence various IT budgets and lines of command," Gertner says.[19]

But Dickerson himself is a unique leader. Like all the best techies, he has a relentless drive to fix problems and improve performance. After all, he comes from an industry that holds as natural law the idea that everything will get twice as good every two years. At the same time, he knows that there is a big difference between the government and Google.

"There's an attitude in the entrepreneurial private sector where we don't care what came before us: We're going to disrupt it," Dickerson says. But you can't just disrupt huge programs at will; you have to innovate with patience. "It will not work, and you will not go far, if you come here with a big attitude, saying, 'You people are stupid, get out of the way and we'll show you how it's done,'" he says.[20] And by bringing this softer approach to the US Digital Service, patiently hacking technology *and* bureaucracy, he found a formula for success.

But the right formula will only get you so far. Ask Dickerson, and he'll tell you that the number one advantage he has is an absolutely top-flight team. With 37 of the nation's best engineers and tech minds, it's no surprise that USDS has made such a splash. But how can you do this in your own agency? How can you build your *own* digital dream team?

BUILDING DIGITAL TALENT

What does your digital team look like?

Gregory Godbout was a man on a mission. He co-founded 18F in March 2014, partly in response to the fallout from HealthCare.gov. With a potent combination of tech savvy and civic-mindedness, 18F was designed to operate much like a tech startup within government, focused on creating best-in-class digital services. But before 18F could fulfill its mandate, they had to find talent. And not just any talent; 18F wanted to build a digital dream team rivaling those from the best technology companies.

"We were looking for mavens and connectors," Godbout says. "The mavens were going to be the thought leaders that would make us 'authentic,' and the connectors were the people who had the connections to get the word out that there was something cool happening here."

A year and a half earlier, Godbout could scarcely have imagined he'd be facing this kind of a challenge. At the time, his main claim to fame was as owner of the popular Arlington Draft House Cinema, a stone's throw across the Potomac from many federal agencies but worlds away in its mission and culture. The path from cinema owner to co-founder of 18F came via the Presidential Innovation Fellows (PIF) program, launched by Todd Park, the federal CTO, which assembled top innovators from the private sector, nonprofits, and academia to spend a year on federal problems such as procurement reform.

Godbout wasn't selected for the PIF program because of his experience with movie theaters; he was also a veteran Beltway technology consultant who had some big ideas for changing government IT practices. "It frustrated me that everything being built for government, all the work projects we were touching, just weren't high quality at all," he says. "And it [is] so easy to build quality today."

At its launch, Godbout and a core group of PIF and CFPB veterans formed the nucleus of 18F. Realizing its audacious vision required a quick expansion of the core team without sacrificing quality. But just as Burton experienced earlier at CFPB, Godbout soon was hindered by restrictive federal hiring rules. "You're so eager and then you come in and you're hit with the wall of the reality of the situation," he explains.

So before trying to hire more people, Godbout and his team decided to reengineer, or "hack," the government's hiring process. Their approach moves candidates through the different phases of the recruitment cycle very quickly—at least by government standards. First, résumés are graded based on two criteria: technical expertise and the ability to work in teams. This winnows the field; promising candidates move forward to the "pitch" phase.

The primary aim of the pitch phase is to understand a candidate's motivation for joining the team. Shortlisted candidates are evaluated foremost on whether or not they're a good cultural fit. "It's not tied to the actual function or even what we think they're going to work on," explains Godbout. "We ask, are they a cultural match?"

This new approach paid off. Hiring times were slashed from six to nine months to six to nine weeks, and the team is determined to shave even more time off of their process. This helped speed up recruitment and enabled 18F to scale up much more rapidly than before. The team grew sixfold in just five months, from 15 people to more than 90. "We were hiring people in weeks," recalls

Godbout. "Federal CIO shops and cabinet departments were calling me saying, 'You did that? How did you do that?'"[21]

But hiring rules are only one part of the problem. Many government leaders should ask a more basic question: How can we attract this kind of talent?

In his book *Drive*, author Dan Pink lists three elements that motivate people to work for an organization: autonomy, mastery, and purpose.[22] Governments may not always be able to compete on salary, but they do have purpose in spades, which represents a huge competitive advantage that matters to many professionals today. The sheer scale of government projects and the direct impact they can have on neighborhoods, cities, or even the nation is nearly unmatched.

"How do you compete on compensation? How do you compete for talent? I think we have a unique value proposition that others don't have," says Jay Nath, chief innovation officer for the city of San Francisco.[23] "We don't have stock options, right? But we do have purpose and meaning. I think that for the right person or for certain types of people this is very attractive." This is particularly true for millennials, 77 percent of whom say they always take an organization's purpose into consideration before joining.[24]

Civic-minded people are prime targets for government. "If the technical foundation is there, you can build on that with mentorship and partnering up people," says Godbout. "But if you don't have that civic-minded, 'rah, rah, I need to do this and I am so into it' attitude—you can't really teach that piece, and we weight that piece a bit more here," he says.

Fixing the hiring process and appealing to purpose and mission are good first steps, but they're still not enough to attract top digital talent. "You could recruit people into a bad environment,"

Godbout says. "Those people would tell their friends and things would fall apart after that. It's not enough to just recruit."

Another point: If you want to truly transform government, the tools you use can't be antiquated. "We use GitHub, and that's a symbol to people—that we're using the latest things," Godbout says. "We use Slack to communicate with one another. That too became a symbol for people being hired. I can't tell you how many people we hired who said to me, 'Once I heard you guys were using Slack….' It just meant that we were cutting-edge, that the tools we use are cutting-edge."[25]

The work environment also matters. "People need autonomy over task (what they do), time (when they do it), team (who they do it with) and technique (how they do it)," writes Pink.[26] Telecommuting, flexible hours, casual dress codes, and a flatter org chart are all standard operating procedures in the tech world. Not so much in most governments. This needs to change to attract and retain the best digital talent.

"We had a 34 percent vacancy rate when I came in; now it's 5 percent," says Chris Cruz, the deputy CIO of the State of California about the California Health Care Services' IT department, which he used to run. The difference, says Cruz, was the adoption of a very aggressive telecommuting policy ("you have to work around [employees'] schedules") and substantial training opportunities in new technologies.[27]

Say you solve all of these problems. Once you have your ideal team in place, how do you make sure they stay in government? 18F's answer: you don't. Its leaders have a refreshingly different take on retention: They don't believe in the idea of a "40-year career" in government. They acknowledge that people will come into government to achieve specific missions and may move on when the job is done.

"With these types of people, you can bring them in for a short period of time, a year or two years, and they're going to need to be highly engaged and high-functioning at all times," says Jennifer Tress, 18F's director of hiring operations. "When that level of engagement runs out, they're going to want to go, and that's okay."[28]

Across the Atlantic, Fiona Dean echoes that sentiment. Dean, who leads digital services for the London Borough of Camden, says, "We picked people that I thought were going to add value to the program and basically encouraged them into it, so I ended up with a bit of a dream team." But, she adds, "What you're creating is a temporary dream team—people will come and go."[29]

Godbout, who calls himself a "serial entrepreneur," is focused on transferring his wealth of knowledge to other government agencies. He left GSA to build out the digital team at the EPA.[30] "We're going to try to scale it. Set it up as a separate business unit, but related to 18F," he says. "And then we're going to launch that service. And for me, that's the closure, right? That's where I kind of took it full circle."[31]

SCALING DIGITAL CAPACITY

Building a digitally savvy workforce

Suzanne Butler works in the UK Department for Work and Pensions' (DWP's) Fraud, Error, and Debt Division, where she manages an IT team. She's also the 100th student to graduate from the Digital Academy, DWP's innovative training endeavor.

The Digital Academy in Leeds, where Suzanne trained, is a lively space. It has the feel of a modern startup rather than a traditional government department. Rainbows of colored Post-it notes cover the walls as students brainstorm ideas and learn the secrets of creating an exceptional user experience. They sift through mountains of Lego blocks, building models and prototyping. The goal is learning how to work in an agile way. Starting with the basics—defining "digital" and the Internet, creating a basic webpage, etc.—cohorts of civil servants work their way toward understanding and practicing more complex aspects of digital tech and service delivery over a six-week course.

As well as technical expertise, academy graduates also take away large doses of digital culture—working collaboratively in a flat, multidisciplinary team, for instance, and putting the customer at the heart of their work.

While she learned many digital tools and techniques, the most important thing Butler took away from the Digital Academy is customer focus. "The customer is definitely at the heart of it," she says, "since everything that you're producing should be driven from the customer or the user. Almost as soon as you get into a discussion about what the customer wants, you know you need to take a step back and go out and do some user research." She characterizes the academy as "busy and visually vibrant, with a different kind of buzz."

The Digital Academy is the brainchild of Kevin Cunnington, recruited from Vodafone to lead DWP's digital transformation. After almost three decades in IT and telecom, Cunnington says he was drawn to government by "the opportunity to do some good after spending most of my life in the commercial sector." Passionate about open-water swimming, Cunnington loves challenges; choppy water at near-freezing temperatures is just one of them. It's the same drive that led him to join the DWP. "For me, it's the challenge that really makes it compelling," he says. "The challenge and the scale of what we're trying to achieve."

Scale may be an understatement. With more than 85,000 employees, DWP delivers critical services including pensions and child care, disability, and ill-health benefits to more than 22 million customers each year. It pays out £166 billion annually, accounting for a third of all daily banking transactions in the UK.[32]

But, unlike many transplants from the private sector, Cunnington isn't intimidated by the department's massive scale. "A lot of commercial organizations are bigger," he says. "They have exactly the same issues of bureaucracy and politicking that big government organizations have. The nice thing about DWP is it only operates in one country, in contrast to my past life at Vodafone."[33]

Early on, Cunnington realized that DWP had severely under-invested in people and digital technology. It had a notable shortage of digital skills, including user research, user experience, analytics, content design, and service architecture. And he couldn't afford to hire enough new digital talent in a reasonable time frame to create the widespread cultural change so sorely needed.

So Cunnington instead decided to embark on the massive challenge of building the department's digital capabilities from the ground up and the inside out. Borrowing from his private-sector work, he created a boot camp–style academy similar to one he'd established previously at Vodafone.

DWP's Digital Academy is designed to get staff members digital-ready, quickly and efficiently. Employees spend six weeks at one of two Digital Academy locations, in Fulham or Leeds, training on key elements such as user-centric design, agile development, and digital government services. They learn wireframing, paper prototyping, agile project management, design thinking, coding, and more. At the end of six weeks, they're shipped back and given a chance to work on actual projects.

And no, six weeks of training *doesn't* mean these freshly minted academy graduates can hit the ground running and manage digital programs. "What you get in six or eight weeks is not going to get you to where you can drop in and lead some of these programs, where we're trying to deliver complex, world-class solutions in a very short space of time," says Rick Stock, the academy's former program director.[34] Instead, Cunnington and Stock created what they call the "plumber's mate" model, in which graduates will know enough to contribute to a team, but not necessarily to lead a project or work independently. From there, they can learn as apprentices until they are ready to strike out on their own.

Stock, known as "Ponytail Rick" because of his long mane of brown hair, designed the academy's curriculum with the help of a few colleagues. Having invested about 10 hours of development time for every hour of training content, he proudly says, "We are the academy—it runs through our veins." Stock had no prior experience as a formal trainer, but says spending 15 years in digital industries proved critical to this challenge. "The handy thing was having had quite a broad experience during that time," he says. "I had a lot of contacts we could bring in."

What really distinguishes the Digital Academy from traditional training models is that it's targeted directly to the kinds of digital roles people are actually seeking, from service architects to user-experience designers to digital product owners. That focus helps graduates learn and speak the same language as experts in their roles.

"They'd come back and say to me, 'Well, we thought we were going to be lost but because of what we learned in the first four weeks, we could sit in a scrum meeting or in a product meeting,' and we knew exactly what was going on,'" Stock says. "That was really a lightbulb moment."

Another critical feature of the Digital Academy has been its focus on learning by working on live projects. Co-located with the Leeds Academy is one of DWP's digital transformation hubs, which houses teams working on live projects, some of them including academy students and graduates. "What we're saying now is, 'Okay, if you're coming through the academy, you've got to have a place to go at the end of it,'" Stock says. "Often, it's one of the projects that are running in the hub. You've got a pipeline effect there."

So far, the Digital Academy has delivered promising results. "This year, we trained up about a thousand people, roughly. Next year's target is 9,000," Cunnington says.

By any measure, six weeks is a long time to pull productive employees away from their daily jobs. Cunnington admits it hasn't always been easy, but "you have to determine what's important and provide the executive support to get on with it," he says.

Ultimately, the goal is not to just focus on hubs and academies, but transforming the whole of DWP. With the philosophy "transformation is a team sport," the DWP is working to achieve the delivery capacity they need by both building skills within the department, and also recruiting into the Transformation Hubs. "All organizations are looking to attract the same talent, so our brand has to be attractive to those people," notes Andrew Besford, head of business design at DWP. "At the moment the recruitment process could be improved, and once we get people through the door, we need to genuinely empower people and not just pay lip service to empowerment, leaving people tied up in governance loops," he adds. DWP plans to work with local universities to get people with the right skills to work on digital services.[35]

BUILDING YOUR DIGITAL TALENT ECOSYSTEM

Tapping into the best digital talent to create public value

The most mature digital governments have strong internal capabilities but also foster deep engagement with the external tech community.

Governments can greatly improve their access to digital talent by participating in the broader tech ecosystem, including "borrowed talent" (contractor employees), "freelance talent" (independent, individual contractors), and "open-source talent" (people who can be engaged to help you solve a problem or create a product). By taking advantage of this ecosystem, government can tap into the skills and talent of those doing cutting-edge work in digital technology, wherever they reside.

This is critical because there will always be more tech talent outside government than in. As tech guru Bill Joy said, "No matter who you are, most of the smartest people work for someone else."[36]

The US Department of Energy (DOE) took this to heart when it sought to solve a vexing solar energy problem. Getting homeowners and businesses to switch to solar power isn't simply a matter of installing more solar panels on houses and office buildings. Other issues, such as grid connection, permitting, installation, consumer education, and financing represent nearly 65 percent of the cost of solar power in some states.[37] As it worked toward solutions, DOE realized consumer and enterprise software applications would be essential to accelerate the broader adoption of solar power.

In 2014, DOE launched its SunShot catalyst program, which called upon consumers, energy companies, entrepreneurs, and startups to develop solutions for the solar marketplace. The program was the brainchild of Michael Contreras, who came to DOE from NASA's Jet Propulsion Lab, where he'd worked on mission concepts to deploy large solar power arrays in space.

"With the catalyst program, we were trying to draw attention to an untapped market opportunity in the very unsexy field [at the time] of solar energy software startups," Contreras says. "I saw my role as akin to an innovation manager. I must have talked to 100 or more people to come up with the approach we eventually used."

After opening the contest and receiving 140 business cases, Contreras and his team selected 17 of the most promising and asked each to build what software-speak calls a minimum viable product (MVP), a product that can reach early adopters and allow you to see what features they like and what more they want. There was only one problem: DOE had neither the capacity nor the technical skills to build a software prototype at the pace that a startup would, let alone 17. So Contreras turned to Topcoder, a crowdsourcing platform for computer programming with more than 900,000 top-tier developers, to work with the teams as they built their prototypes.

"We have a community that's sizable enough that we don't have to worry about finding the right people, and we have consistently been blown away by the talent," explains Michael Morris, part of the founding team of Topcoder. "Originally we just couldn't believe how good the people were. And coming from the technology field, all of us were like, wow—very impressed, and humbled."

To start, DOE capitalized each SunShot Catalyst team with $25,000 in Topcoder challenge budget. Teams could spend these funds through Topcoder, engaging with developers that filled gaps in to build their software-based solutions. Each task, module, design, or solution on Topcoder is structured as a challenge, and the $25,000 provided enough funding to cover anywhere from 8 to 12 challenges per team. The challenges could be used to obtain everything from app design to back-end development and testing.

"We have a number of different challenge types, and this is where Topcoder is unique," Morris says. "Your project is like a giant Lego block that we break into smaller parts; this is called atomization. We have to know how to break the system down into its pieces."

Using this model, DOE had 17 working MVPs in nine weeks, products that could be put in front of users to see which might actually increase solar adoption.

One of the startups participating was Solar Site Design, led by Jason Loyet. His firm's mission is to drive down customer acquisition costs, which represent nearly 10 percent of the soft costs of solar installation. The catalyst program enabled his start-up to build the second generation of its customer acquisition platform. "It was really fast paced," says Loyet about the process. "I was amazed at how quickly it all moved. In the dot-com era it would take millions of dollars and months or years to put together what they were able to do in a matter of weeks."

It's a radically different model than the standard government approach—studying the issue to death and then issuing an RFP or a grant. "We were two times faster than standard Phase I Small Business Innovation Research (SBIR) grants and 10 times cheaper than SBIR's Phase II grants," Contreras says.

Across the Pacific, the New Zealand government engaged digital startups to help solve another critical business issue: the huge costs businesses face interacting with government. The Ministry of Business Innovation and Employment, NZ (MBIE), and a handful of other agencies partnered with incubator and accelerator CreativeHQ to launch the R9 Accelerator, a 12-week innovation program modeled after startup accelerator programs. The R9 Accelerator was designed to grow raw ideas and concepts into viable, creative solutions to reduce by 25 percent the costs and efforts businesses face complying with government rules, regulations, and responding to RFPs. The program's approach centers on co-design and co-delivery of services with the private and public sector collaborating to develop better public services.[38]

Cross-sector project teams prototype and co-design their minimum viable products (MVPs) and then test their ideas with real customers. VizBot, the output of one of the teams, is a digital platform that simplifies the process of obtaining licenses and permits for construction companies. The online portal allows companies to submit application forms, view requests for clarification notes (RFC), and respond to requests for further information (RFI). The tool also includes a central dashboard to track applications and provide visibility into the process.[39]

Incentive prizes and challenges, which will be discussed in chapter 4, and hackathons offer other promising models for tapping into the external ecosystem of top-notch digital talent. Hackathons' focused nature brings forth solutions that governments may struggle to evolve in isolation. A case in point is New York City's Big Apps competition, which released city data to participants and encouraged them to develop mobile applications that use municipal data to solve citywide problems. The winners of the 2013 challenge included apps to identify healthy options at nearby restaurants, help parents find quality child care, calculate homeowners' savings for a range of solar-power options, and teach kids about software coding.

BUILDING YOUR TEAM

Our global survey of government leaders identified workforce issues and technical skills as the most challenging areas for digital evolution. Many government agencies lack the right skills to take advantage of digital transformation—skills in user research and analysis, agile and iterative project management, financial modeling, and digital supply chain issues, as well as coding and design. They need a plan that pinpoints the capabilities they need and suggests ways to secure them.

As the examples in this chapter demonstrate, hiring, retaining, and training the right talent requires new approaches to recruitment, training, and engagement with the wider digital talent ecosystem. It will require offering the best candidates something beyond compensation and benefits and creating a workplace in which they can thrive.

CHAPTER 2 PLAYBOOK

DEVELOPING DIGITAL CAPACITY

LEADERSHIP STRATEGIES

Go on a recon mission. Before starting with anything digital, go out and spend time learning what's really going on within the organization. Getting a feel for what you need, what's standing in your way, how things are being done, and what needs to change can provide clarity and direction for your next move.

Start small and move fast. Starting with something basic like redesigning a website may seem unsexy, but it can lay the foundation for more complex things. Ultimately, you may need the support of people who need to *see* change before they can get behind it so small pilots and quick wins can get you the buy-in and employee support you need.

Practice digital aikido. Digital-savvy leaders shape and build energy on digital platforms rather than resist them. They use digital media to gauge attitudes, build influence, and motivate action through social networks. Leaders can use digital aikido to assess the moods, opinions, and motivations of people within online social systems, and tailor their moves accordingly.[40]

Servant leadership. Shift the mentality from top-down to servant leadership. "IT managers need to have a mindset of servant leadership, in that their primary job is to clear away obstacles to getting things done," says Mark Schwartz, CIO of the US Citizenship and Immigration Service, "because in truth, the only people who are actually adding value are the developers and testers. They're the ones who actually do something that produces a product that people care about. Anybody that's not a developer, tester, or involved in product creation is there to support them."[41]

TALENT STRATEGIES

Create interesting job descriptions. Government is notorious for dry, boring job descriptions with mind-numbing titles like "internal directives administrator" or "senior level information technology specialist." Instead create alluring job descriptions like this one from the USDS:

> "Our engineering leads drive technical teams to build large-scale, innovative products that serve the American people. You need to be an expert strategizer, fixer, and builder with the engineering chops to roll up your sleeves and push your own code. You'll provide leadership on major technology projects, manage project teams with focus and vision, contribute to product strategy, and support strong teams of engineers."[42]

If you absolutely must retain the official job descriptions, put the fun ones on top and then create a forum to excite people.

What's your offer? Create a unique value proposition to attract the best talent. Talented people care about what they do. Government employment may not come with stock options and fat paychecks like the private sector, but it does offer purpose and an opportunity to affect millions of lives. Make that your value proposition and speak from the heart about your team's mission.

Don't leave recruitment to HR staff. You'll never get the team you need unless you get personally engaged in recruiting. To find the right people, you have to hunt for them. This means using unconventional recruiting tactics, advertising in the right places to get the attention of top talent, and tapping into your networks. While recruiting for digital roles, look at attributes beyond hard skills such as motivation, cultural fit, working style, and passion.

Embrace a temporary dream team. In an age when workplace rules are evolving and the "gig economy" is a reality, it's unrealistic to expect top technologists to have decades-long careers in government. If you have the chance to cherry-pick and build a digital team of brilliant individuals, take it—even if it's temporary. This dream team can lay a lasting foundation for digital transformation by putting in place the right processes, culture, structure, and dynamics that the organization will benefit from in the long term.

Balance tech whiz kids with government veterans. The best digital teams are multidisciplinary and diverse. The shiny new technologist from Silicon Valley cannot come in and save the day without the people who have the domain expertise and government savvy. You need the best of both worlds—those with a deep understanding of government's processes and challenges as well as innovation-minded tech whizzes—to collectively transform government processes and programs.

Identify capabilities gap. Prepare for digital transformation by addressing digital skills gaps and investing in resources and technologies to help build a culture and capabilities supporting the digital transition.

Ensure cutting-edge technology for cutting-edge talent. You can't expect digital maestros to work on archaic tools and blow-hot, blow-cold Wi-Fi spots in the office. Getting the digital team equipped with cutting-edge IT and technology infrastructure is a prerequisite to building the team.

Identify the torch-bearers. Recruiting the right talent goes beyond process and requires a human touch. Some call them mavens and connectors, but whatever the name, you need to identify people who will spread the word both within and outside the government about becoming part of your digital team. These are generally the people who are at the top of their game, have credibility in the market, and believe in the agency's mission.

Build a digital talent ecosystem. It would be difficult to match all talent needs through recruitment only. Tapping into an external digital talent ecosystem could mean bringing in temporary talent from the private sector through partnerships or asking the developer community to solve specific problems through prizes and challenges. The bottom line: Head out and explore innovative channels for your talent needs.

TOOLS AND TECHNIQUES

Digital maturity diagnostic. Many organizations have challenges preparing and adapting to digital. A digital maturity model creates a holistic view of the organization and strategic approach to digital transformation.

Digital transformation roadmap. Build a roadmap that covers key areas such as culture, leadership, workforce, and procurement. Detail how to engage stakeholders and secure their backing to implement the strategy. Describe how procurement processes could be reformed for the digital delivery of services.

Digital fellows program. Launch short-term design and technology programs to attract top-notch web designers and developers. To attract top talent, use everyday language to describe the opportunities and illustrate the nature of the work and why it would be important and impactful.

Digital academy. The UK Department for Work and Pensions (DWP) created a boot camp–style digital academy to train and upskill staff and get the organization ready, one cohort at a time. The staff is trained on key elements of digital technology such as user-centric design, agile development, and digital government services.

Prizes, challenges, and hackathons. Sometimes governments will have to tap into an external ecosystem of top-notch digital talent. One way would be to initiate prizes and challenges. Another effective way of getting the developer and designer community involved is through focused hackathons.

RESOURCES (WEBSITES, BOOKS, AND OTHER COOL STUFF)

The US Digital Services Playbook is a treasure trove for executives seeking to understand and navigate the digital journey. Each digital play comes with a short explanation and checklist to follow through. [https://playbook.cio.gov/]

The Government Digital Service (GDS) in the UK has created a detailed matrix of the skills needed to create, maintain, and improve digital services and information. The skills are categorized across government functions: digital specialist, agile delivery, procurement, service management, etc. It's a good starting point for executives to identify the skills required in their organizations. You can find the matrix here: [https://www.gov.uk/government/publications/digital-and-technology-skills-matrix].

The Code for America Fellowship Program: The program teams up experienced technologists with local governments to work full-time for a year in partnership with government officials to develop innovative digital approaches to delivering key public services. [https://www.codeforamerica.org/governments/fellowship/]

The National Association of State Personnel Executives (NASPE) study on state government IT workforces includes recommendations on the future of IT staffing and delivery structure. [http://www.naspe.net/assets/docs/Research-and-Publications/nascio_itworkforce_underpressure.pdf]

A report from the Alliance to Transform Government Summit contains key drivers, barriers, enablers, and solutions frameworks for digital transformation. [http://www.naspe.net/assets/docs/Alliance/transforming-gov-summit-report0714_f1.pdf]

Taking a leaf out of the CFPB book, explore job portals that are frequented by your potential recruits.

- Stack Overflow Careers [http://careers.stackoverflow.com/employer]
- GitHub job listings [https://jobs.github.com/positions]
- CrunchBoard [http://www.crunchboard.com/]
- Dice [http://www.dice.com/]

For good books on digital leadership, try *The Adventures of an IT Leader* by Robert D. Austin, Richard L. Nolan, and Shannon O'Donnell and *Innovative State: How New Technologies Can Transform Government* by Aneesh Chopra.

CHAPTER 3

HACKING DELIVERY:
Design and Execution in the Digital Age

On October 1, 2013—the day HealthCare.gov made its disastrous debut—14 states plus Washington, DC, launched their own health care exchanges.[1] Connecticut, with its Access Health CT exchange, was one of them. The stakes couldn't have been much higher for the Constitution State.

"I remember the night before launch people working very late," the former Access Health CT CEO Kevin Counihan told *Vox*. "I brought in pizza and two cases of red wine, and that increased productivity about 30 percent. I didn't sleep too well."[2]

In the days—and weeks—before the launch, the IT team worked around the clock, fixing problems, redoing code, testing, and then testing some more, preparing for an unknown number of visitors that could range anywhere from thousands to millions. "People would sleep in the office on beanbags," recalls Newton Wong, the consultant who drove the go-live process. "We were surviving on big buckets of peanuts and cheese puffs."[3]

The team planned for the worst—making sure they were prepared for however many visitors came through the digital door on day one. "Our biggest worry was that we'd get slammed on the first day, so we wanted to be ready for that," Wong says.

One way they prepared for the launch was to turn their system on a few days early and ping the federal hub to iron out the inevitable integration issues. "I was flabbergasted that we were told we couldn't test earlier in production, so when we found out it was up, we started testing it with real data," says Jim Wadleigh, the then CIO of Access Health CT (and now CEO). "We found a bunch of things that allowed us to handle errors better."[4]

All the preparation paid off. "We flipped the switch and god-dammit, it worked," Counihan proudly recalls. "We started looking at screens and saw people coming on the site and traffic growing and growing. Some people were getting a little emotional and high-fiving. It's really a day I'll never forget." On day one, the site accommodated 45,000 unique visitors and more than 430,000 page views.

In all, the Connecticut launch performed admirably, never going down once, while HealthCare.gov and many state exchanges experienced catastrophic problems, including full system crashes. Six months in, 198,000 Connecticut residents had signed up for Access Health CT—one of the highest per capita sign-up rates of any state—and amid all the chaos, Connecticut (along with Kentucky) emerged as one of the most successful models for an online health insurance exchange. "Was it perfect? No," says Wadleigh. "But while other states were having volume and scaling issues, ours was working."

Good people can agree or disagree on whether Obamacare was a good idea, but it's a debate beyond the scope of this book. The purpose here is to answer a narrower question: Once Congress and the administration decided to launch the health insurance exchanges, why did Connecticut's online exchange succeed where so many others struggled and often failed—and what does this tell us about how governments can successfully deliver digital initiatives?

To get to this answer, we have to return to June 28, 2012, when 14 states, the District of Columbia, and the federal government began creating the health care exchanges that would allow US citizens to find mandatory health insurance as part of the Affordable Care Act (ACA).

The immediate question was how and how *well* the various exchanges would work. The stakes were enormous. Success or failure would determine whether millions of uninsured Americans would be able to sign up for coverage. And the effort would be highly visible, with wide-ranging and serious political implications.

By any measure, it was a profoundly ambitious undertaking. Exchanges would have to be user-friendly, accurate, and powerful enough to accommodate a flood of traffic upon launch. That didn't leave much time. "We had to do a three-year implementation in 10 months," says Wadleigh.

Despite the high stakes and short time frame, Connecticut had a few distinct advantages in building its exchange. For one thing, it had a management team deeply experienced in large-scale IT rollouts that understood health care. "[Hartford] is the insurance capital of the world," says Wadleigh. "As you look at our entire leadership team, we come from the Cignas, the Aetnas, the Uniteds, the Health Nets, all those companies. That is probably what's helped us be so successful. We understand health care."[5]

In contrast, many states' teams were filled with policy people. "The states that were successful understood that the rollout was a big IT project, not a policy project," explains Wadleigh, who credits his experience with big digital launches at Cigna and MassMutual as essential for the health exchange rollout.

Connecticut also benefited from its commitment to a basic and easily accessible platform. While many states saw serious scope creep in the months leading up to the launch, Connecticut delayed some of its website's more complex features until after the launch.

"Over the Christmas holidays in 2013, I went through require-ment after requirement and pulled out everything that wasn't necessary for the go-live," Wadleigh says. "We ended up deferring 40 percent of the project." In hindsight, even the tight time frame did more good than harm by forcing much faster decision making than is typical for government.

Another of Connecticut's key design decisions was that Health Access CT wouldn't require individuals to log in before checking for eligibility and options. The federal site and many state sites required users to begin by creating an account, which created a huge bottleneck.

Testing was another key to success. While other states and the federal government were still in the construction process, Connecticut was testing and refining, over and over. "We had an August 1st due date to start testing and come hell or high water, we were going to start testing then," recalls Wadleigh. The team did virtually every kind of testing and war-gaming needed to address glitches and prepare for contingencies, including user testing, acceptance testing, stakeholder testing, and reliability testing.

In contrast, the federal site and some of the other state sites went into production with little or no testing because develop-ment was delayed by slower decision making and poor vendor management.

"At the root of all this is governance," explains Wadleigh. A big component of the leadership team's governance approach was to avoid confirmation bias by bringing a diversity of opinions and expertise into every aspect of the project. "I trusted nobody," says Wadleigh. "I had different PMOs, different staff, different vendors all involved."

In another smart move, Counihan and Wadleigh intention-ally set low expectations for the debut, publicly warning that it could be bumpy. In one prelaunch press release, Counihan said: "We know there will be defects that we will continue to uncover as we roll out this system to residents."[6] It was a savvy decision. "To be frank, I viewed it as a survival period," Counihan explains. "My goal was to get through open enrollment with as little customer disruption as possible and to make sure we earned the ability to start patching the system up in the summer of 2014."

Health Access CT demonstrated that governments *can* execute complex, high-profile, time-sensitive digital projects. Unfortunately, one of the reasons it received national attention was its status as an anomaly in a sea of troubled launches. But Connecticut's insurance exchange proved that competent digital delivery is an attainable goal.

Getting there is a three-stage process. The first is *design*: You imagine a new way of delivering a service or pursuing a mission with digital technologies, through design thinking and user-based research. The second stage involves *delivering* on the design, through prototyping, agile development, extensive testing, and multiple iterations. Finally, you must *operate* the new digital service, staying close to the customer and using analytics to continuously hone it.

THE DESIGN STAGE: IMAGINING A NEW FUTURE

Rethinking and reimagining service delivery should always begin with the user rather than the existing program. This means focusing foremost on citizens' actual needs and touch points, even if they don't fit or reflect your current operating model. This requires understanding what design really means—and the difference between good and bad design.

75

Sometimes poor design is obvious. Consider, for example, London's infamous glass skyscraper at 20 Fenchurch Street that, due to its unusual parabolic shape, ended up damaging roads and melting parked cars with focused sunlight.[7] But more often, bad design is so familiar it's hard to spot. The QWERTY keyboard, which dates from the 1870s, continues to dominate in the digital age due to habit, despite the existence of more ergonomic and easier-to-use alternatives such as DVORAK.

Today, though, in business and increasingly in government, there's a growing realization of the importance of design in everything from customer experiences to societal problem solving.

"Design is an approach to problem solving," says Hillary Hartley, deputy executive director at 18F. "It's how you think about something. It's not the typefaces; it's not the pixels. Design is what makes a product successful. It's the thing that makes it useful, that makes it understandable."[8]

Since its inception, 18F has emphasized and adopted a design-focused and user-centric way of working. They've incorporated a technique called *protosketching*: Designers and developers build a rough prototype in three hours or less by sketching in code as well as on paper. Even if the protosketch is imperfect or outright unusable, it gives teams and clients something concrete to examine and elevates the discussion to issues of data, design, and functionality.

The United Kingdom's Government Digital Service mirrors 18F's approach, articulating its vision through 10 concise design principles based on actual user needs:[9]

1. Start with needs (user needs, not government needs).
2. Do less.
3. Design with data.
4. Do the hard work to make it simple.

5. Iterate. Then iterate again.
6. This is for everyone.
7. Understand context.
8. Build digital services, not websites.
9. Be consistent, not uniform.
10. Make things open: It makes things better.

Today, this is how the United Kingdom undertakes all of its digital projects. But that wasn't always the case. Kathy Settle recalls that during the Gov.uk transition, as they were moving 312 websites onto the Gov.uk domain, they initially relied on department personnel to explain users' needs.

Unfortunately, "quite often the organizations weren't in direct contact with their users, and their articulation of user needs reflected that," Settle explains. "Things were built on the basis of what people *thought* user needs were. Some of it turned out to be wrong."[10]

Interaction with end users adds a depth and authenticity that's essential to good design. The simple practice of observing how a user actually works during an average day can sometimes yield more useful information than hours of interviews. The idea is to walk a mile in the user's shoes—or get as close to their experience as possible.

USER-CENTERED DESIGN IN PRACTICE

So, how do you understand train travel? You ride the train.

When Amtrak decided to redesign its customer experience— then including three online portals, each with a distinct audience—

it made sure the redesign focused entirely on the user. This involved a brisk and geographically expansive research project.

In the course of a few weeks, teams of "user experience" researchers rode Amtrak trains across the United States, interviewing passengers and staff and visiting stations along the way, covering the Northeast Corridor, the entire Pacific coast, and the South from New Orleans to Houston. Two weeks and more than 100 interviews later, the team had uncovered valuable insights, witnessing problems firsthand.

"You hear that certain areas are broken.... [W]hen they say something is working well, it's because they have workarounds that are completely counterintuitive to someone who's actually designed a digital platform," says Mark Waks, one of the project researchers. "But you need to see that to know what it is that's actually broken."

For example, customers contacting Amtrak call centers *could* get a quick cost estimate for travel on any route. The researchers learned, however, that call center workers were jotting down customer requests on paper and generating estimates with a calculator. Behind-the-scenes information such as this can direct you to areas in dire need of transformation.

In short, user research reveals what structured interviews may not: that a seemingly one-dimensional problem can have hidden layers.

User *validation* is also critical in designing a better experience, which is why agile design is so helpful. Testing prototypes with actual users at every step helps gauge how well a problem has been addressed. "In products where we employ digital, we bring in users every step of the way as much as we possibly can,"

Waks says. "Otherwise, you're basically just judging it on your own personal perceptions, not the users'."[11]

The design stage is in many ways a blank canvas on which organizations can define their ambitions based on their resources and goals. Some will take a more expansive approach, completely rethinking how services are delivered, while others will pursue smaller projects, such as allowing citizens to upload forms and documents via mobile apps. In either case, the key is to understand users by studying their behavior, and to design approaches to reduce or eliminate the pain points you've observed.

Let's start with a relatively simple example. Determining eligibility and applying for government benefits can be time-consuming and frustrating. It typically involves finding and scanning payroll forms and birth certificates and carrying or faxing them to multiple offices. If you've ever applied for a home mortgage, you have a sense of what this can entail.

In 2011, the Texas Health and Human Services Commission (HHSC) simplified this process by installing a statewide integrated system that aggregates eligibility for various federal and state programs by using an integrated rules engine. This allows a single mother, for example, to apply for multiple benefits with one application. The system rules assess the programs for which she may qualify based on her income, household size, and other factors.

With more people from all income levels becoming comfortable with mobile transactions, HHSC began exploring how it might bring its integrated eligibility functions to the mobile arena. Older models of IT development might have entailed a multiyear, multimillion-dollar effort to build a mobile-friendly version of the service.

Instead, HHSC focused on the user perspective, asking what would eliminate a pain point for users but also benefit the agency. Unsurprisingly, one problem applicants often cited was the need to submit verification documents. While they could do so by mail, fax, or the web, many applicants didn't have easy access to scanners or personal computers. Perhaps surprisingly, however, many *do* have access to smartphones with cameras.

Since banks have long allowed their customers to deposit checks by taking a picture of the paper check with their phone and hitting the upload button on an app, why couldn't applicants do the same thing? HHSC's team knew it was technically possible. But would applicants actually use such an app? And what kind of experience would attract the most participation?

These aren't the kinds of questions we can answer in advance. They require time in the field, talking with real users. In HHSC's case, it meant spending time in the service centers that many applicants visit when applying for benefits.

There, HHSC's designers learned a lot about the people they hoped would use the app. Most benefit applicants did indeed have smartphones, but their devices were often a generation or two behind and thus lacked advanced capabilities. This turned out to be a critical piece of information in designing the app. Most were intimately familiar with their phones' capabilities because it was their primary means of connecting to the web. "Many users were used to conducting their business on mobile devices instead of personal computers, making them sophisticated users," explains Stephanie Muth, the deputy executive commissioner at HHSC who spearheaded the project.

The team introduced its first set of wireframes to users just two weeks after the project began. Demand was high; applicants quickly snapped up the software. The team gathered valuable information from early users that helped them refine the user experience and design features to be included in later builds.

In a few short months, the agency released the app in the iTunes and Google Play stores. Almost immediately, the mobile versions took off; within a month, mobile document uploads surpassed those from desktops. A few months later, the app had been downloaded 300,000 times. And HHSC released five versions in the first year alone, each with additional functions and a better user experience.

Several lessons emerge from this experience. First, don't make assumptions about how those who are less fortunate use—or don't use—technology. Instead, *test* your assumptions with real users and continuously ask them for feedback. Secondly, start small and get a minimum viable product to users as quickly as possible.

If Texas's HHSC project occupies the easy end of the complexity spectrum, Amtrak lies at the other. HHSC wasn't imagining entirely new benefits or creating a program from scratch; it simply wanted a more efficient way to enable self-service.

Amtrak's attempt to reinvent its services with an entirely new brand and customer experience is far more ambitious. What if customers could access Amtrak with desktop, tablet, and mobile devices? What if they could use an app to request an Uber ride, reserve a table or seat, order and pay for meals, purchase amenities, and even receive alerts for sights to see along the journey? Amtrak found answers and added them to its redesign.

"We're selling a journey, an experience, and not just a ticket on a train," says Deborah Stone-Wulf, VP of sales distribution and customer service at Amtrak. "It has taken us a bit of time to understand that, but we do understand it, and that's where we're headed."[12]

In this sense, Amtrak's transformation relative to HHSC's is akin to comparing telescopes and microscopes: The components and processes may be the same, but differences in scale and objectives change everything.

AGILE DELIVERY

With 29,000 employees, Transport for London (TfL) is one of the world's largest transit agencies, operating everything from the iconic London Underground and red double-decker buses to the city's ferry system. In summer 2015, TfL was in the midst of a huge modernization effort that included, among other major changes, removing the booths that separate TfL employees from passengers in the subway stations. The idea was to free up space for more concessions while providing better, more intimate customer service.[13] This "Fit for the Future" initiative was controversial; many TfL employees objected, for instance, to offering late-night service. Such factors made the change-management program particularly challenging.

One thing was certain, though: If TfL workers were to be out among Tube passengers providing assistance, they needed mobile access to all the information they had had in their booths—and more. That's where Conor Maguire, who directs TfL's mobile program, came into the picture.

Maguire's job was to bring to life the concept of a customer service assistant (CSA) circulating among passengers, equipped with the latest technology and mobile applications. "We have a service we need to provide within the stations, and we have customers that are going to want to get information," Maguire says. "We're not going to have an office space, and so there are already some boundaries you work within. Then you work from that point and say, okay, how are we going to model the service? How are our users going to work in that environment?"

Acquiring hardware for the CSAs was the easy part. Thousands of devices were acquired from the London Summer Olympics, which had "ambassadors" helping visitors navigate the games with tablets and smartphones. Ultimately, TfL distributed more than 10,000 mobile devices, including tablets, smartphones, and specialty devices, to its workers.

The harder part was determining the capabilities the devices should actually have. Ideally, they would allow employees to work from virtually any location, providing better situational awareness, data sharing, and customer service.

To decide which mobile abilities would be most transformational for its workforce, TfL adopted a user-driven, agile approach—a big departure from how it typically ran IT projects.

"Traditional business process engineering starts from a place of, 'Let's capture all the *as is* and then create the *to be*,'" Maguire says. "You end up with an approach several degrees away from the real world and real users."[14] Instead, his team interviewed many different employees, researched their work processes and habits, and developed "personas" and journey maps.

This allowed TfL to move mobile CSAs from concept to reality in a relatively short period. Through user research, interviews, and constant requests for feedback, concepts were developed and tested quickly and effectively.

WHAT IS AGILE DEVELOPMENT?

Agile (adj.): able to move quickly and easily

In 2001, a group of like-minded developers and software industry leaders developed the Agile Manifesto. Their aim was an alternative approach to software development that mitigates the risks and loopholes of the traditional waterfall approach. Their alternative approach, called "agile," was built around four core values:

AGILE APPROACH CORE VALUES		
Individuals and interactions	over	Processes and tools
Working software	over	Comprehensive documentation
Customer collaboration	over	Contract negotiation
Responding to change	over	Following a plan

FROM CONCEPT TO DELIVERY: DEFINING THE APPROACH

Maguire insisted on using user-centered design and agile delivery to develop new apps, but his decision met with some resistance. One of the initial opponents was Alistair Montgomery, a systems solution manager for operations who worked closely with Maguire on the mobile program.

Montgomery was a TfL veteran, point man for many of TfL's major IT upgrades, and saw his job as making sure proposed technology changes were actually a good fit for the agency and its employees. Having spent years using "waterfall" development for IT projects, Montgomery was far more comfortable in the world of Gantt charts and deliverable timelines. When Maguire first proposed that they use agile development for the project, he was deeply skeptical.

"I was set in my ways," he says. "I thought [agile development] was a gimmick filled with buzz terms and would never work. There were no Gantt charts. No plan. No set delivery. And when I heard about the 'scrum masters,' I said, 'Come on, this is ludicrous.'" Fortunately, Montgomery says, he was outvoted. "Within two weeks, I was a complete convert," he recalls, laughing. What changed his mind? "It was fun," he says. "There was no hierarchy—it was all peer to peer—and I could see progress quickly. That's why people have been won around to this."

Agile development won over Montgomery, but more importantly, it convinced his bosses. Previously, they never actually saw a new technology until after it launched, meaning they were investing millions of pounds based on plans and Gantt charts. Agile development was totally different. "We threw up a wireframe, personas, prototypes," Montgomery says. "It just clicks. They can see immediate progress."

By making progress more visible, agile development helped Maguire and his team build significant trust with TfL leadership. Montgomery says, "One of the instructions we got from senior executives was, 'We want you guys to keep doing what you're doing as you're doing it. Just keep going. We believe you.'"

FEATURES OF AN AGILE PROJECT: THE SCRUM

The "scrum" is one of the most useful tools of agile development. It involves three distinct roles for staff.

Product owner: A link between the client and development team; also an active member of the team, engaged in iteration, planning, and review. The product owner is a representative from the customer side who can clarify questions arising during the development cycle.

Scrum master: The coach or facilitator—but decidedly not the boss. Generally, a peer with the knowledge and expertise needed to guide the project through bottlenecks and impediments.

Team member: Each team member is a specialist and brings critical skills.

Development and testing in scrum occur through short bursts called "sprints" generally lasting for two to four weeks. During sprints, "artifacts" are used to make the process visible to the development team. These include user stories, product backlog, and sprint backlog.

User stories: User stories are short, simple descriptions of a feature expressed from the standpoint of the user or customer. They help turn user requirements into tasks.

Product backlog: Product backlogs assemble user stories in one place, breaking them into small chunks and prioritizing them based on the most important stories or requirements.

Sprint backlog: A subset of the product backlog, this is the team to-do list for the span of the sprint.

THE SPRINT CYCLE: RUN, RINSE, REPEAT

A typical sprint cycle includes five steps:

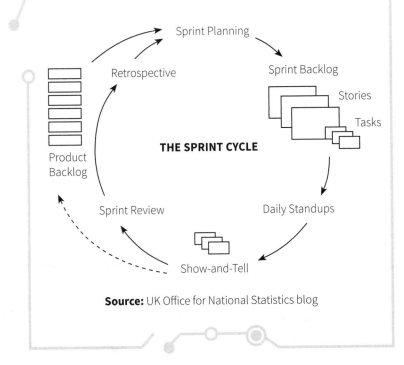

Source: UK Office for National Statistics blog

1. **Sprint planning:** User stories picked from the top of the product backlog are cut into manageable chunks and added to the sprint backlog. The planning involves two basic parts: what we'll do and how we'll do it.

2. **Standups:** Daily 15-minute meetings in which each team member reports; the aim is to monitor progress, identify issues and remove roadblocks.

3. **Sprint review:** At the end of each sprint cycle, the work product is reviewed. A "show-and-tell" provides a way to examine the actual product and its functionality.

4. **Retrospectives:** This step focuses on the process, what worked and what didn't, and how things could be improved.

5. **Repeat:** Any new stories arising from the sprint review and retrospectives are fed back into the product backlog and prioritized. The full cycle then repeats.

In fact, executives liked seeing the regular deliverables so much that it caused a bit of a problem. "I would walk out of the meeting and get a phone call asking, usually a couple hours later, if I can push that app to their device, despite the fact they've only just seen a wireframe," Montgomery says, "because they want to show it to someone."

MAKING AGILE DEVELOPMENT WORK FOR GOVERNMENT

Agile development is by no means new. Nor is it unproven; according to the Standish Group, agile projects are 350 percent more likely to be successful than waterfall development, and *600 percent* more for very large projects.[15] Despite this track record, agile is still used only sporadically in government. And when agile projects interact with parts of government not used to the methodology, they often meet resistance.

"The most frustrating thing for me is that I see agile development working really, really well, but we haven't got the full agile system throughout the rest of the process," Montgomery says.[16]

This issue is no small problem in government. The public sector can throw up significant barriers to the adoption of user-centric, agile technology development. In the *2015 State of Agile* survey, respondents cited organizational culture as a leading barrier to agile adoption.[17]

Most government IT executives have spent their entire careers in waterfall development. They value knowing (in theory, at least) the "as is" and carefully designing the "to be." Political and constitutional structures can make it seem risky to use agile methods—how can you begin without knowing your final delivery model?

Agile's focus on the user, rapid iteration, and frequent change represents a *huge* shift and often encounters resistance. Executives and political leaders alike, however, are slowly accepting that the waterfall method often involved a completely inadequate vision of the "to be." In practice, during the course of any project, dates almost always slip and designs tend to be watered down.[18]

In contrast, the agile philosophy is to accept the uncertainty and push ahead with something modest as quickly as possible to gain rapid user feedback. But culture can be hard to change in large organizations.

Fortunately, thanks to voluminous research in the field of change management, today we know a lot about how to address such cultural barriers. Two of the more interesting thinkers on the subject are Chip and Dan Heath, authors of the best-selling book *Switch: How to Change Things When Change Is Hard*.[19] They argue that we spend too much time trying to make the best *analytical* argument for change, when what we really need are better *emotional* appeals. In a conversation with Chip, he explained it to me this way:

> I love the analogy by Jonathan Haidt at the University of Virginia. He imagines the analytical side of the brain that decides we want to change something as a tiny human rider riding on top of a big, emotional elephant. I love this metaphor because it gets the relative weight classes right. If you think you're going to think your way into change, that's the tiny human rider on the big emotional elephant. In any direct contest of wills, the elephant is going to win. It's got a six-ton weight advantage.[20]

Instead of beginning a change effort with a 100-slide Power-Point presentation, then, think of how you can appeal to the emotional side of the brain. In the case of agile development, as TfL's Montgomery discovered, the best way to convert skeptics is to engage them in the process. The UK's Government Digital Service (GDS) has institutionalized this approach through a method it calls "learning agile by doing." GDS encourages career civil servants to participate in agile development to really learn and internalize the approach.[21]

The learning-by-doing approach can help dispel some of the common myths about agile methods. One is that *agile means no planning*. In truth, detailed planning is as essential to agile as it is to waterfall development. At the start of each sprint, a planning meeting takes place to achieve agreement on user requirements. The daily standups are used to define each day's activities in high detail. For complex projects, careful planning drives the architecture and the operating model. Yet it's still perfectly possible to work in an agile manner while making commitments to milestone dates and planning for external dependencies.

Another popular myth is that *agile means no documentation*. Agile development produces documentation—it just differs from that of waterfall. Instead of a single, voluminous list of requirements, the team creates a set of user stories that can be iterated and updated on the go.[22] Learning by doing helps familiarize and win over critics to this different but highly effective approach.

The Heaths recommend starting small and trying to quickly highlight bright spots. "The key thing for me was to demonstrate something, get a quick win," Maguire explains. "Be a bright spot; make yourself visible as an agent of change that is really delivering some great stuff."[23]

DIGITAL OPERATIONS: DELIVERING A FIRST-CLASS CUSTOMER EXPERIENCE

It became the stuff of late-night comedy when Jon Stewart jumped on the story, but it was no laughing matter.[24] When the sad saga of long waits and deceptive scheduling practices at the Department of Veterans Affairs facilities in Phoenix began unfolding in spring 2014, it included allegations that as many as 63 veterans had died while waiting for appointments.

A subsequent VA Office of Inspector General investigation couldn't substantiate these allegations, but its report made it abundantly clear that there were serious problems with scheduling backlogs and overloaded care providers within the VA.[25] Within a month of the scandal breaking, VA Secretary Eric Shinseki tendered his resignation, leaving behind a sprawling organization—including 150 hospitals and more than 800 clinics serving around 6 million veterans—in disarray.

As the story unfolded, it became painfully obvious that the VA's service problems extended well beyond Phoenix. A follow-up investigation by the VA inspector general examined nearly 100 different VA sites across the country suspected of falsifying scheduling records to hide months-long delays for appointments.[26]

The fundamental cause of the problem wasn't in dispute: The system was being overwhelmed by veterans returning from Iraq and Afghanistan.[27] But the scandal uncovered other problems at the VA, not least of which was a 1980s-era computerized scheduling system the agency had repeatedly failed to replace.[28]

Another chronic issue was fragmentation. With more than 1,000 websites, 956 help-line numbers, 42 call centers, and 220 separate databases, you can easily imagine the frustration among veterans.[29] Where do you even start?

In August 2014, under new leadership, the VA launched MyVA, an ambitious program to create a personalized, customer-centric customer experience providing veterans with the best possible care in a timely fashion. Ultimately, the VA leadership would like to align the department's entire budget around the veterans' customer experience. "Our goal is simple," says VA Secretary Robert A. McDonald. "Provide quality medicine and first-rate health care with the same proactive, real-time, courteous, coordinated service as the top-ranked customer service companies in the country."[30]

On the way to this goal, the VA hopes to change how it interacts with veterans. VA's databases are fragmented; there's no common source of veteran contact information. The agency believes that one key element in improving its service is to eliminate the clients' need to provide the same information multiple times. A unified digital experience will require a common data interchange and a way to combine thousands of public and private organizations into an integrated ecosystem.

In September 2015, the VA launched the beta version of Vets. gov, a site intended to serve as the single point of contact for any information and services veterans may need. Within a year, veterans would be able to create a single account on Vets.gov with all their personal information. Built on the tenets of human-centered design and agile development, Vets.gov documented its approach through an open playbook.[31]

"Our process building Vets.gov will be one of constant refinement and improvement. Your feedback will guide and shape everything we do. That's as it should be. This site isn't about us— it's about you," promises McDonald in his message to users.[32]

At the core of the MyVA transformation is the understanding that it's easier than ever for customers and organizations to stay connected. The department is shifting its focus to building relationships with its customers before *and* after a transaction occurs.

Many in government hope this mentality spreads throughout the public sector. "We're the country that created Amazon, Facebook, Twitter, and the Internet," US chief technology officer Megan Smith told a conference in January 2015. "Why shouldn't [government] websites and mobile services and the way that we do customer service with the American people—why shouldn't they be that good?"[33] A scientist and former Google executive, Smith hopes that government agencies someday can match the private sector in improving customer experience with digital services.

Phaedra Chrousos, the General Services Administration's first chief customer officer, is even more ambitious. "I hope we can keep up and don't just do the Amazon of today, but the Amazon of the future," she says.[34] Her team spent five months mapping the entire GSA customer experience and conducting research to better understand their needs.[35] For Chrousos, customer feedback—good, bad, or ugly—is essential to an improved customer experience. "I want them to know we're listening and that we're collecting their data and that we really care. Keep complaining—but complain to us," she says.[36]

Through GSA's Voice of the Customer program, Chrousos and her team worked to understand the customer experience. They learned that one of the most challenging aspects of improving the customer experience is often a lack of good data about customers.[37] The team also found each GSA program focused on its own clients without considering that multiple programs may have common customers, creating an opportunity to collaborate to serve them better.[38]

Many other agencies have created chief customer officers, a diverse group highlighting the fact that the desire to improve customer experience spans many different domains within government.[39]

SENSE AND RESPOND: USING ANALYTICS AND FEEDBACK LOOPS

Agencies that deliver digital services need to talk to their customers—and more importantly, they need to *listen*. Whether through customer feedback or analytics, digital services must be attuned to changing customer needs, responding with minor tweaks or entirely new versions depending on demand. And building a functional digital service is only part of the puzzle; to scale, operate, monitor, and optimize it is just as critical.

In Finland, for example, city planners visit local parks just after snowfall. Looking at the footprints in the snow, they identify the paths people naturally take in the absence of a pre-existing one. These "desire paths" are mapped and can be paved in the summer.[40] For digital services, this is a powerful metaphor. With analytics and feedback loops, organizations can uncover desire paths and use the data to improve their services.

Consider Gov.uk. After a mammoth redesign, the site now successfully hosts the services and information for more than 300 organizations. "Gov.uk is the total of thousands of little observations," says Matthew Hancock, cabinet minister and paymaster general and successor to Francis Maude. Highlighting iteration as one of the guiding principles for digital transformation, he says, "Iteration means basing decisions as much as possible on observation, not prediction."[41] In the eyes of its creators, Gov.uk isn't finished yet—and may never be. According to the GDS, "it's a continual work in progress which will adapt and improve all the time to better serve the needs of all its users."

In the US, all federal websites now use Google Analytics for Government. The Office of Federal Procurement Policy (OFPP) launched its Acquisition 360 program with a rating system fed by feedback from contractors and vendors. This Yelp-like system consists of three surveys for different audiences that operate on a "very satisfied" to "very dissatisfied" scale. "In addition to getting feedback on how well the acquisition team worked, we are also interested in better understanding why contracting officers choose certain interagency solutions over others, or why they choose certain contract vehicles," said OFPP Administrator Anne Rung in a memo on the subject.[42]

Public bodies then need to act upon what they've learned. They must sift the evidence of user feedback, complaints, system logs, and web analytics, evaluating what they see and prioritizing their responses, sometimes trading improvements policymakers want for those users demand.

This is the model adopted by VicRoads, the road and traffic authority for the state of Victoria, Australia. Residents visit its site for a laundry list of activities, from registering their vehicles to learning about road safety rules. With a million visits each month, it's the second-busiest government website in Victoria. With those kinds of numbers, a website that isn't user-friendly could translate into millions of unhappy voters.

Despite its visibility, however, as of 2014 the VicRoads website hadn't been overhauled in five years. It had become overwhelmingly complex and delivered a fatally disjointed user experience. Information on the site was difficult to find and understand; transactions would often redirect users through a tangle of separate sites. Furthermore, the antiquated website wasn't mobile-friendly, even though more than 40 percent of its customers used mobile devices to access it. The VicRoads team realized they needed to completely redesign the digital experience.

With a timeline of just 14 months, they began with the heart of their mission: the customer. Employing a host of user research techniques including workshops, journey mapping, and interviews, the team developed a deep understanding of user needs and preferences and also conducted a survey to find out which channels users preferred for different tasks—online (mobile or desktop), phone, e-mail, or service center.

The results were telling: Most citizens preferred the online channel but expected to be able to complete transactions on any device. Users also became more task-focused on mobile devices, meaning they didn't want to be hindered by peripheral information; they just wanted to get the job done. They were visiting the VicRoads website not for a relationship but to do something, as quickly as possible.[43]

To make the site's dense content more digestible for mobile users, rewrites were critical, even though they hadn't been a part of the original plan. "We had not initially planned or budgeted for rewriting content," explains Jolanda Zerbst, web services manager at VicRoads. "There was initially some resistance from content owners to condense information due to concerns about legal consequences of not having all that information there."[44]

But when senior stakeholders were shown an example of a page rewritten to be more mobile friendly, with 66 percent less content, they expressed support and provided the go-ahead and resources for a redesign.[45] The site redesign optimized web pages irrespective of the device used, delivering a consistent experience across platforms.

Also instrumental to a seamless digital experience was the practice of phased releases. Instead of releasing a new app as soon as it was finished and crossing their collective fingers hoping it would work, administrators would release content to beta groups and internal VicRoads staff to gather feedback on bugs and issues and suggest additional features.

Once that phase was finished, new features were subjected to rigorous A/B testing before general release. For example, 95 percent of site visitors might see the old change-of-address form, with only 5 percent able to use the new version. Only after addressing any remaining issues would the application be opened up to all users. "These are critical services, so potentially the consequences could be fairly nasty if we get this wrong," says Jason Hutchinson, a project consultant. "A/B testing was a great way to ensure that whatever we release worked before we released it to everyone."[46]

The website's redesign transformed the user experience. "I changed my address on my license using the VicRoads website and it took 30 seconds," one customer said. Adaptive tests that never ask the same question twice help learners study for their driver's tests. With performance analytics, VicRoads can understand how its services are being used and areas needing improvement.

The customer focus was a game-changing component of VicRoads' redesign. "We're caring for our customers and users, and it's really about thinking, 'If they're trying to do something, how can we make it as easy for them as possible, and if it's not going to be a nice experience, how do we help them through that experience?'" Zerbst says.[47] The goal is to focus on improving the experience for customers, whether it's a single transaction or long-term interaction.

This need to understand user needs and create workable feedback loops will continue to grow. The rise of the Internet of Things will have a significant impact: As governments aggregate the outputs of sensors, beacons, and other devices, employees won't have to go out and count footprints in the snow—their systems will do that for them, freeing them to create value from the data. In this sense, we're just beginning to scrape the surface of the possible.

PUTTING IT ALL TOGETHER: A BILLION-TO-ONE EXPERIENCE

Digital delivery based on the three phases discussed in this chapter—design, delivery, and operation—can create customer-centric, billion-to-one (B2ONE) experiences across government. B2ONE involves a set of core digital capabilities that will enable fundamentally new ways of delivering value to citizens:

Data—aggregated data form a critical component of B2ONE models. Organizations can use the data and brains of the crowd to provide highly customized experiences.

Sensing—sensing, digitization, and analytics offer unprecedented abilities to gather and assess evidence in real time. With Google Analytics, agencies can aggregate and analyze data on user preferences to improve their services. More broadly, sensing encompasses a huge variety of data useful to government, such as roadside traffic sensors, health-monitoring devices, thermostats, motion detectors, and more.

Behavioral analysis—analytics monitor *actual* consumer behavior, providing much more accurate and actionable data than questionnaires. Behavioral science, which studies how the way in which choices are presented can influence behavior, can in turn transform such data into effective action.[48] In 2013, for instance, the Gov.uk publishing team found that a small change to a web page—adding the bright red logo for NHS organ donation—significantly increased its number of donor sign-ups.[49]

Adaptation—a world-class customer experience requires strong feedback loops with users. This means collecting data on user behavior, constantly gathering feedback, and using it to continually improve products and services. Philadelphia's Philly311 app, for example, interacts with citizens in real time. The app has overtaken all other media to become the primary channel for citizens to communicate with the city.

"We're constantly gathering data from customers as to what's working and what's not working in our operations with all of our channels, so that we can make the appropriate changes; otherwise, nobody's really going to use it," says Rosetta Carrington Lue, Philadelphia's chief customer service officer. She attributes a large part of the app's success to the city's follow-through on user feedback.[50]

Organizations that develop these capabilities will differ from predecessors built for a different age. As noted in chapter 2, most large organizations today were born out of value-chain theory, which puts customers at the end of a process that converts inputs into products or services designed to meet their *assumed* needs. But as we now know, digital ecosystems don't work this way: Rather than being at the end of the value chain, customers should be engaged *throughout*, often acting as both suppliers and customers in the same value exchange.

AltSchool, a San Francisco–based network of K–8 schools, has a simple mission: to redefine the value chain for education, using technology to offer more personalized learning experiences.[51] At AltSchool, students' learning plans adapt to their changing needs while providing and receiving constant feedback on personal progress. Computerized tests are adjusted for individual skills; parents are constantly asked for feedback.

"We are trying to actually advance a new model of a school," says AltSchool CEO Max Ventilla. "Rethinking school starts with rethinking curriculum, and we've reimagined how students should be spending their time in and outside the classroom."[52] While it's still in its infancy, AltSchool shows that B2ONE can disrupt even the most traditional value chains, such as those in education.

But what about something like mass transit? Can we personalize bus transportation? Dynamic bus routes are already being used in Boston and Washington, DC, where a transportation startup called Bridj uses analytics to move commuters to their destinations. Instead of fixed routes, Bridj assesses where passengers live, work, and travel to offer personalized options. The app works simply enough: You enter your destination and the time you'd like to leave and reserve a seat. Then you receive directions to a place where a Wi-Fi-enabled Bridj bus will pick you up.

The confluence of the crowd, big data, and customer empowerment is shaping new business models that behave more like ecosystems and self-managed networks than traditional value chains. This environment is fueling a new breed of commercial, government, and social entrepreneurs who engage customers and citizens in the design of experiences that can adapt to changing circumstances.

CONCLUSION

Delivery in the digital age ultimately depends on how governments execute each stage of the process (design, deliver, and operate); it's simply the sum of its parts. Services designed around the user, powered by systems built iteratively, tested rigorously, and operated in response to changing customer needs, will be truly transformational.

This kind of innovation could become commonplace in government agencies, whether it's the VA or Transport for London.

The key is to exploit the B2ONE capabilities of big data, sensing, personalization, adaptation, and behavioral insights. The most digitally adept governments will *imagine and design* the future by meshing their business goals with user-centered design and a good understanding of current technologies. They'll *deliver* the future by adopting agile methods. And they'll *run* the future with a culture of continuous feedback and analytics-driven insight.

DESIGN AND EXECUTION IN THE DIGITAL AGE

DESIGN STRATEGIES

Use internal tools to encourage good design. Many middle managers aren't overly concerned with how an external website looks or functions, but most would love to have their lives made easier through better internal tools and apps. Starting with these can be a great way to demonstrate the value of good design.

Get out of the office and talk to real users. Firsthand knowledge of user needs and behavior can yield priceless design insights. Effective design is based on observed facts, not assumptions.

Decide the scale of your transformation. Based on your goals and resources, determine how big or small changes should be. Are you rethinking how a service is delivered or simply building a user-friendly mobile app? Gauge what and how much user research you need, and how much time and effort it will involve.

DELIVERY STRATEGIES

Learn by doing. Changing the way things have always been done can be an uphill climb, especially in the public sector. How do you get skeptics on board? By encouraging them to try the new approach and learn as they go. Whether it's agile sprints or design thinking, a hands-on approach can improve understanding and debunk myths and prejudices.

Show, don't tell. Letting stakeholders play with something tangible, even if it's not perfect, helps them see the impact the digital product could have.

Modify agile for large projects. Traditional agile is designed for small teams working on well-defined projects over short periods of time. Scaling agile to large government IT projects involving dozens of teams over multiyear time horizons requires adapting the approach. Key modifications include: multiyear roadmaps, more time spent in discovery and design to define the overall scope, coordinating cross-team dependencies, consolidated reporting, and increased testing.

OPERATIONS STRATEGIES

Use feedback loops to drive continuous improvement. Data analytics and user feedback provide opportunities to tweak and fine-tune services as well as the entire customer experience. A "sense and adapt" approach based on constant iteration can deliver truly transformational value.

Deliver an experience, not just a service. Take advantage of the sensing and analytical capabilities of modern digital systems. Instead of one-size-fits-all approaches, look for ways to achieve useful customization for different users.

WELL-DESIGNED DIGITAL SERVICES REQUIRE A STRONG CONNECTEDNESS BETWEEN:

- **Ambition and scale**: The desired level of transformation given the scale of the challenge/effort.

- **Experience**: The human interactions, emotions, and influences that drive engagement.

- **Operational evolution**: Changes to the organizational structure, effectiveness of employees, and change management required to adapt operations.

- **Engagement platforms**: Engagement platforms that support and connect the technologies necessary to enable customer experience and value.

TOOLS AND TECHNIQUES

Customer journey map. Journey maps document the entire as-is process, both good and bad. Journey maps should be based on robust user research and should address the customer's reactions before, during, and after using the service.

Experience blueprint. This is another tool to illustrate and analyze the end-to-end customer experience. It's a logical next step after the customer journey map that connects the interactions that make that journey possible. Critical questions to ask while building the blueprint: What does the customer expect from the experience? What steps are required to deliver it?

Customer engagement plan. The customer engagement plan uses the journey map to understand opportunities to engage the customer across the journey. It involves a three-phase process: attract, engage, and extend. *Attract* focuses on customer needs. *Engage* provides recommendations customized to individuals through behavioral analysis. *Extend* consists of customized communications and goal- and event-driven alerts that prompt easy action.

Prototypes. These are used to define and validate concepts. Sketches, paper types, visual comps, clickable prototypes, and integrated proof of concept are five types of prototypes, with a sketch being the lowest-fidelity and an integrated proof of concept the highest. Use them wisely based on your requirements.

Protosketching. This is where design meets coding. Building prototypes takes time, but protosketching can be done in hours and provides a concrete way to review issues involving data, design and functionality. It's a great tool to bring to a meeting when you're trying to gain stakeholder buy-in.

Agile metrics. For large, complex projects, agile dashboards enable program leadership to track metrics across multiple scrums and see the comparative performance of the scrum teams.

RESOURCES (WEBSITES, BOOKS, AND OTHER COOL STUFF)

The GDS and 18F blogs discuss strategies and problems involved in developing government digital services. A few resources are presented below, but both blogs offer a wealth of useful information. Visit: [https://gds.blog.gov.uk/ and https://18f.gsa.gov/blog/].

The GDS Service Design Manual is a collection of guides and resources for different organizational roles, including service managers, content designers, and chief technology officers. It also describes the different service design phases the GDS employs. [https://www.gov.uk/service-manual]

DESIGN RESOURCES

The GDS provides a list of 10 design principles foundational to digital development. [https://www.gov.uk/design-principles]

18F provides a one-stop shop to learn about its design principles and structure, as well as materials you can use for training and workshops. [https://methods.18f.gov/assets/downloads/18F-Method-Cards-beta-Preview.pdf]

Usability.gov is a good resource for user-experience best practices and guidelines. It provides useful refreshers on user research methods and user-centered design, as well as federal-specific resources. [http://www.usability.gov/]

The US Web Design Standards provide open-source user interface components and a visual style guide for creating consistently superior user experiences across federal government websites. [https://playbook.cio.gov/designstandards/]

AGILE RESOURCES

The Agile Manifesto website provides a quick reference to the values and principles of agile software development. [http://agilemanifesto.org/]

18F offers a quick guide for running a three-sprint agile workshop. [https://18f.gsa.gov/2014/10/21/how-to-run-your-own-3-sprint-agile-workshop/]

Mike Cohn's *User Stories Applied for Agile Software Development* is essential reading on developing user stories. The "Writing Stories" chapter is available online. [http://www.mountaingoatsoftware.com/system/asset/file/259/User-Stories-Applied-Mike-Cohn.pdf]

Scrum: A Breathtakingly Brief and Agile Introduction is a summary of a much larger book, *The Elements of Scrum* by Chris Sims and Hillary Louise Johnson. The summary, available online, provides a quick overview of scrum roles and tools and the sprint cycle. [http://www.agilelearninglabs.com/resources/scrum-introduction/]

Scaling Agile at Financial Institutions: Lessons from the Trenches, provides an overview of how some institutions have scaled agile successfully and some of the challenges that executives have to consider. [http://www2.deloitte.com/content/dam/Deloitte/us/Documents/financial-services/us-fsi-agile-at-scale-brochure.pdf]

OPERATION RESOURCES

The Digital Analytics Program (DAP): Digital Metrics Guidance and Best Practices offers a trove of information on understanding digital metrics: measuring, analyzing, and reporting on the effectiveness of your web, mobile, social media, and other digital channels. It's a good starting point for developing your strategy to measure performance, customer satisfaction, and engagement. [http://www.digitalgov.gov/services/dap/dap-digital-metrics-guidance-and-best-practices/#part-4]

CHAPTER 4

HACKING PROCUREMENT:
Building Better Avenues to Procure Digital Services

Mark Schwartz, chief information officer of the US Citizenship and Immigration Services (USCIS) agency, remembers what it was like to work in a startup. "When you're CIO of a small company, you have urgent needs, and you just have to get capability out very quickly," he says. "You don't have time to build huge programs and go through long oversight cycles."[1]

You can imagine his surprise when he arrived at USCIS in 2010. Early on, he asked to have a few small changes made to a web page. He was told they would take *a year* to complete. Standing in the way of the simple changes was something called MD 102: a couple of hundred pages of guidelines on how the agency should procure, develop, and test software. "It's absolutely brilliant," Schwartz says sarcastically. "If you wanted to instruct a large group of people that they must use the waterfall approach, you couldn't possibly write it better."

Written in the wake of the September 11 terrorist attacks, MD 102 prescribed an agonizingly slow process designed to meet the needs of 22 separate agencies and 104 congressional oversight committees. "It's total chaos," says Schwartz.[2]

Spoiler alert: Schwartz threw out the guidelines, made up his own policy, and did 100-some releases within a year. Most government employees and leaders can probably relate to both his initial frustration and his determination to blow up the system. The way things stand, if you want to do anything related to IT procurement in government, there is a process you have to follow—and you can expect it to move at a glacial pace.

THE SAD LEGACY OF GOVERNMENT IT PROCUREMENT

You would think that a system this slow and this careful would produce very few failures. Not so. If anything, it's just the opposite. The history of government IT is filled with horror stories of long delays, billion-dollar cost overruns, and software that just plain didn't work.

The marquee example, of course, is HealthCare.gov. The *New York Times* summed it up well: "For the first time in history, a president has had to stand in the Rose Garden to apologize for a broken website."[3]

Nearly every American took note of the initial HealthCare.gov stumbles. But there are countless other failures, of similar scale, that have gone relatively unnoticed by most of the electorate. If anything, it is surprising that it has taken this long for the nation to receive a Rose Garden apology.

And it's not just government. An entire book could be written on the history of failed large-scale IT projects. Research by the Standish Group, a consultancy that studies software projects, makes clear the scale of the problem. Of all government and commercial IT projects in excess of $10 million, the group found that 52 percent were late, over budget, or unsatisfactory in their implementation, while 41 percent failed outright. Only 7 percent of large-scale projects in either the public or private sector succeeded.[4] These are not the numbers you hope, and expect, to see in an era when most people can buy their groceries on a smartphone.

So what's going wrong? Why is the system so broken? There's no one answer, but it's increasingly obvious that the current method traditionally used for procurement and development—which is essentially a very expensive blind wedding—plays a big role. Winners are chosen not necessarily because they will do the best job, or even a good job, but because they are the cheapest, or have the right mix of small business set-asides, or they know how to navigate the byzantine requirements of a process like MD 102.

Mark Naggar, who manages the innovative new Buyers Club at the Department of Health and Human Services (HHS), describes what happens next. "It's basically, 'Congratulations, you won the award,' then they drop the mic and walk out of the room. And in six months you get something and realize it's not what you wanted, not what you needed."[5] He adds, "So often we're focused on getting something awarded and there's not enough attention focused on implementation."[6] It should come as no surprise, then, that implementation is where most projects break down.

If you're in government, it's easy to feel trapped, to wonder if this system was designed to make your life miserable and keep you from getting anything done. That's how Mark Schwartz felt when he first got to USCIS. But in reality, there's no Dr. Evil laughing as he thinks up new ways to make you tear out your hair (if you still have any). "The people who put together MD 102 wanted to do the right thing and were not a faceless bureaucracy," says Schwartz.[7] But in their attempt to minimize risk, and to make sure that government delivers on its legal and policy needs, they created a process that all but guarantees the opposite. They practically ensured that government would get old technology, implemented poorly, for 10 times the price it should cost.

That's not to say these boxes don't need to be checked. Government has always had unique requirements, and the Internet did not magically make them disappear. But for the promise of digital transformation to be realized, these needs must be met in a smarter, faster, and cheaper way.

Public sector approaches to procurement are rightly designed to make sure that public money is well spent. This must continue, but the risks of poor public spending are not the same as they were before the digital age. The root cause is the accelerating pace of change itself. Historically, change was slower, and there was greater confidence that established ways of working were stable. Within that business model, the procurement practice across the public sector was to deliver services as cheaply as possible.

This favored long-term supplier contracts and low unit costs. It also had the effect of freezing business models at the point in time that IT is bought, suppliers are selected, and processes are established. And yet, in the digital age, nothing could be less desirable. This is an age of exponentially rapid change, where business models of five years ago are rendered obsolete by smartphones, big data, connected sensors, and more. Public procurement must change to reward innovation and flexibility.

Government officials are overwhelmingly frustrated with both the commercial inflexibility of their organizations and the unresponsiveness of their vendors. A significant number of vendors have footholds in the public sector that are threatened by digital transformation. Governments need commercial strategies to free themselves from lock-in and to move to lower-cost options for all kinds of services—whether digital or not.

PRINCIPLES OF A REINVENTED PROCUREMENT SYSTEM FOR THE DIGITAL AGE

What does digital-age procurement look like? Innovators across government are starting to piece together an answer, pioneering more agile and lightweight models with success. Six common themes are emerging from these efforts:

1. **No blind marriage—instead, deep courting.** Innovators are ditching the blind marriage in favor of getting up close and personal with contractors. They've shortened request-for-proposal (RFP) time periods, asking vendors to focus instead on creating working prototypes so evaluators can try them out. Unlike traditional procurement, this system is more show than tell—the better to see which contractor best meets their needs.

2. **Modular approaches with faster cycle times.** When it comes to IT, government tends to build big programs. Rather than trying to find ways to make these megaprojects run faster, the procurement innovators often use an entirely different approach: They take on very small batches of requirements at a time and push them all the way through to production as quickly as possible.

3. **Bake-offs: Flexible, agile ways to engage contractors.** Today's more innovative programs make flexibility and agility a priority, using a "bake-off"-style approach that involves short-term sprints

and teams from multiple contractors. By not tying themselves to a single company, and by keeping deliverables smaller, agencies can keep their options open and change priorities on the fly.

4. **Using purchasing power to catalyze innovative approaches.** From education to defense and security, government is either a dominant or *the* dominant buyer in many markets. The public sector can use its buying power to shape and create "public sector markets" in ways that deliberately foster lower-cost digital innovations.

5. **Open up procurement through the power of prizes and challenges.** By uniting problems with problem solvers, incentive prizes and challenges have powerful impacts, such as attracting new organizations to compete for government business, stimulating markets, and mobilizing action. This open-sourcing is a powerful antidote to fossilization in all areas of government, including procurement.

6. **Train government buyers in digital-age acquisition.** The private sector has plenty of people who understand how to buy digital services in a fluid market, but the government does not. Training models created by business can help develop a modern, innovative corps of digital government buyers who are savvy about products, process, and the need for speed.

Let's look at each of these themes in more detail.

SHOPPING FOR SUPPLIERS IN THE UK DIGITAL SERVICES STORE

The United Kingdom's new Digital Services Store helps agencies procure agile capabilities. Opened in 2013, the store is a platform where buyers in government can essentially research and "shop" for contractors based on their agile capabilities. The store includes hundreds of suppliers who have been pre-evaluated and categorized, making it easy to find the right one for specific mission needs. Moreover, it has simplified the procurement process on both sides, giving suppliers one place to offer services and buyers one place to procure.[8]

NO MORE BLIND MARRIAGES: THE HHS BUYERS CLUB

Since he was recruited in 2014 from the federal Centers for Disease Control and Prevention, where he was a lead contract specialist, Mark Naggar has blazed a trail for innovative acquisitions at HHS. "We're looking to shake things up," he says confidently.[9]

While digital innovators typically blame procurement personnel for being intransigent, Naggar is part of a growing number of procurement officials who are determined to be part of the solution instead of the problem. The program he spearheaded, called the HHS Buyers Club, is an internal community where procurement and project managers can collaborate on new approaches. Filled with like-minded innovators, the Buyers Club is not much different from its Hollywood namesake: an unlikely collection of renegades working together to find something that actually works. "We want to solve the problem of failure," he says. "We want to turn around and have success."[10]

Of course, this is easier said than done. But since early in his career, Naggar has been frustrated by how little focus there is on the end user in the design of government IT systems. He knows that a big part of the problem is the "blind marriage" at the heart of most government contracts, and the inherent lack of communication between those procuring, developing, and using technology. So he set out to build a community to address that. "End users really need to drive decisions and be involved in development," he says. "Increasing the success rate requires participation and collaboration by key stakeholders throughout each acquisition, from identifying the problem/need to ensuring deliverables are met."[11]

To that end, the HHS Buyers Club provides a space for members to:

- Test innovative procurement methodologies for IT service acquisitions and share the results for others to benefit
- Develop newer, easier, and more effective acquisition models and processes
- Engage all the key stakeholders with mutually beneficial education and outreach

Like any club, be it Sam's Club or Costco, membership has its benefits. "There's no cost for membership, other than aligning yourself: subscribing to the notion that there are better ways to buy IT services than currently exist. And if you follow that road, and the methods we are espousing and experimenting with, you are going to have better results," says Naggar. "Over time, the current way of doing things has shown an extremely high failure rate. Our method has significantly mitigated that."

While the HHS Buyers Club is open to any new ideas ("We're more concerned about realizing and pushing innovative acquisition methods than about what mechanism you choose," says Naggar), one method has become particularly popular: agile development.[12] The agile process is widely used in the private sector, and incorporates the principles discussed previously. At HHS, Naggar has been leading the way from a waterfall model and toward an agile method in order to accelerate the agency's acquisitions and mitigate risk.

One of the greatest benefits has been effectively taking misaligned expectations out of the procurement process. "Instead of requesting proposals that are purely text based, we now require contractors to provide a minimum viable prototype, so we can actually assess their IT software development capabilities. It's like show-and-tell, as opposed to just tell," he explains.

In one case study, a group at HHS needed a new web content management system. Typically, the agency would procure this software in just one stage, on the basis of proposals that could be as long as 30 pages. However, this is a huge burden on contractors, as well as on the agency itself, which has to review all the proposals that are submitted. So Naggar's team instead used what's called a two-stage downselect approach. How does it work? "In the first stage, all we ask for is an eight-page concept paper and cost proposal," he says. "After selecting five vendors to go on to the second stage, we gave each a $10,000 purchase order, and asked for a revised cost proposal, a 20-page performance work statement, and a prototype."

The process is similar to what the Defense Advanced Research Projects Agency (DARPA) has been doing for decades. The agency operates more like an investment firm than a government agency, rewarding the best and most promising ideas with seed money. DARPA's approach is to ask teams to compete based on an initial design concept. Shortlisted teams are given funding to conduct additional feasibility research or develop their concepts. Based on their conclusions and concept research, teams are once again narrowed down to a select few that receive funding to move to the next phase and develop prototypes of their concepts.

This approach has not just proven to be successful but is also wildly popular. "The evaluators of the program were blown away. They're used to just reading and reading and reading and not really seeing much," says Naggar. "Now they can see which contractor better meets their needs and which one really understands their organization."

Of course, all of this has been shared with the Buyers Club. Procurement and development managers across HHS can read about this use case and study its best practices online—as well as share similar experiences of their own.

MODULAR, FASTER MODELS: THE US CUSTOMS AND IMMIGRATION SERVICE

In the *Star Wars* films, the Death Star was the "undefeatable ulti-mate weapon" that was "brain-meltingly complex and ravenously consumed resources." The first Death Star, as those familiar with the series will note, fired its main weapon only once before being destroyed by a Jedi. The second was much bigger than the first and also had great difficulty firing. "Time and again" throughout the *Star Wars* series, "war-winning weapons tend to be simple, inexpensive, and small."[13]

The problem with the Death Star project was that it was simply too complex for any program manager to properly design or oversee. It was actually technical oversight that made the station vulnerable to attack. In *Return of the Jedi*, Darth Vader even complains that construction is behind schedule.

The above observations, written by Lt. Col. Dan Ward of the US Air Force, highlight the very problem faced by government today. The public sector has become famous for cost overruns and design failures, often because of attempts to build the IT equivalents of Death Stars. Avoiding a similar fate requires finding a way to simplify.

Schwartz concurs. "What tends to happen in our environment, and what we have to fight against, is that we build big programs," he says. "You can't tackle one mission need unless you have a lot of mission needs that you can put together into a program and get it through the oversight and appropriations process."[14] This is the type of project for which lengthy guidelines like MD 102 were designed. The problem is that trying to build and micromanage the electronic equivalent of the Death Star contradicts a key rule of IT: The bigger and more complicated your project, the more likely it is to fail. On top of that, the cycles become much too long, because each individual feature is now part of a complex, multimillion-dollar effort. Just as Schwartz discovered when he first arrived at USCIS, you may have to wait a year for something you could do yourself in a few minutes.

"I think what has kept the old way of doing things going is that it seems, at first glance, to be the *only* way of doing things," says Schwartz. "But it turns out that some of the problems that we have in government can be well addressed by bringing in techniques from the startup world."[15] In particular, Schwartz is also a big proponent of agile development. He moved his agency away from the waterfall method and on to agile almost immediately after arriving. This meant ripping up MD 102 and writing new guidelines inspired by how agile is used in the private sector. At the core was the idea of taking a fast, modular approach to procurement and development. Instead of trying to build large, complex programs all at once, his team would only take on small groups of requirements at a time and push them all the way through to production.

In agile, this is known as a continuous delivery pipeline. "What this lets us do is minimize risk in a big way," says Schwartz, "because all you're really committing to—all you're risking—is a small batch of requirements and time. When you can do that, oversight needs are much less, procurement needs are much less, and everything else follows from there."

That said, it quickly became obvious that for agile to work in USCIS, it would have to meet the unique requirements of a federal government agency. For the past five years, Schwartz had spent most of his time building a pipeline of projects, and then aligning contracting, quality assurance, and security to an agile approach. "I think if we could do this across the government, it would be revolutionary," he says.

Several trends have made it much easier for government to move in this direction. One particularly important new factor is the public cloud. In the old days, you'd first have to order hardware, then build hardware environments, and then set them up with a data center. You'd also have to get procurements processed—all of which leads to long and expensive development cycles. Now a new environment can be set up in seconds in the public cloud. "We can do something with them, if necessary, and turn them right off again—and we have spent almost nothing," says Schwartz. "It's a huge enabler for breaking things down into small pieces of work and delivering them quickly into production, so that we can then start immediately tweaking it."

BAKE-OFFS: FLEXIBLE, AGILE WAYS OF ENGAGING CONTRACTORS

Dissatisfied with the traditional model, Schwartz has also been experimenting with new ways of engaging contractors. He argues that large, multiyear contracts don't do much to encourage high-quality work or customer service over the long run. Instead, they put the focus on the award, rather than the delivery. Wanting to turn that model on its head, Schwartz and his team developed a bake-off-style approach they call Flexible Agile Development Services, or FADS. The idea behind FADS is that rather than make one big award, USCIS would make awards to four different contractors for agile development teams. Then it would start the project with two teams from each of the four contractors. Seems simple enough, right? The twist is that every six months, USCIS would readjust the number of teams from each contractor—so if you're performing well, it would add teams from your company, and if you're doing poorly, it would subtract teams, or bring you all the way down to zero. And it would just keep resetting and adjusting every six months. "The contractors feel competitive pressure, and they have an incentive to try to excel and show us what a good job they're doing, because then they would win more business from us," explains Schwartz.

What about competition among the contractors? Wouldn't that be bad for the project? Schwartz and his team had a plan for that. They told the contractors, "We're going to judge how happy we are with your teams, and based on that, decide how many teams to buy from you. And one of the criteria we're going to use in deciding whether we're happy with you is how well you collaborate with the other contractors." So far, Schwartz says, that has led to a positive dynamic: "There's a lot of energy, a lot of contractors stepping up to help other contractors, just to show how collaborative they are."[16]

Since they aren't governed by long, detailed contracts, Schwartz and his team can change priorities on a dime. The modular approach enhances this even further. "Sometimes we get political things that come down, or something becomes important all of a sudden. We can shift gears in no time," he says. "And people love that."

USING PURCHASING POWER TO CATALYZE INNOVATIVE APPROACHES

From elementary and secondary education to defense and security, from transportation to health care, government is either a dominant or *the* dominant buyer in many markets. At $500 billion annually, the US government is the world's largest purchaser of goods and services—to say nothing of the purchasing power of state, provincial, and local governments around the world. Intentionally or not, the public sector is already the 800-pound gorilla in many markets today.

Given its size, the public sector can shape the markets in which it operates by taking cues from the private sector. For example, Walmart used its enormous buying power to deliberately shape the entry of products into new markets—and thus help drive down the costs of household goods for rural America. Similarly, the public sector can use its buying power to shape and create "public sector markets" in ways that deliberately foster lower-cost digital innovations.

Take law and justice. For decades, less crime and better safety meant tougher sentencing laws, which in turn led to massive increases in funding for incarceration. As of 2015, 2.4 million people, one in every 100 adults, were behind bars in the United States. Lower-level offenders have accounted for a significant portion of the growth in a prison population that has more than quadrupled since 1980.[17] Electronic monitoring has the potential to break the trade-off between more prisons or more crime. By removing low-level offenders from prisons and putting them under house arrest, electronic monitoring enables governments to dramatically reduce their spending on incarceration ($5–25 per day compared with $79 per day for prison).

Another example is in education. Digital learning and "blended" learning, which combines digital resources and traditional classroom instruction, cost a fraction of the all-traditional approach. During the last decade, the National Center for Academic Transformation has worked with hundreds of public universities to redesign individual courses around a blended model of education that takes greater advantage of technology.[18] These course redesigns have covered all sorts of disciplines, from Spanish to computer science to psychology. They typically incorporate digital learning tools—simulation, video, social media, peer-to-peer tutoring, and software-based drills—as well as some classroom lecturing. The average cost reduction has been a whopping 39 percent, with some course costs reduced by as much as *75 percent*.[19] All in all, the cost of delivering a four-year degree via online curriculum only (with instructors) is less than $13,000, compared with $28,000 and $106,000 at typical public and private institutions, respectively.[20]

If policymakers wanted to revolutionize education and decrease costs, they could grow the market for digital and blended learning by redirecting existing funds from traditional models.

This, after all, is the same model the Pentagon used to grow a distinctly disruptive innovation: unmanned aerial vehicles, or drones. The US Air Force now trains more "joystick pilots" than fighter and bomber pilots combined. Why? Drones incur just a fraction of the costs associated with manned aircrafts and satellites, but they can improve key performance capabilities such as flight longevity while putting no pilots in harm's way.

Another way to encourage disruption is to create institutions outside mainstream government agencies whose purpose is to foster and leverage cutting-edge technologies for public services. DARPA, with a mission of dramatic and disruptive innovation, clearly plays this role for the US Department of Defense. It is small, flexible, and tightly focused on the goal it wants to achieve.[21] The agency uses research teams from academia, industry, and the federal government, across a variety of disciplines, to drive its results and move research quickly to the marketplace.

Operating in this fashion, DARPA has yielded many staples of modern military and civilian life. It has funded the development of everything from the Internet in previous decades to cheap, small satellites that can be put into orbit for one-third of the cost of traditional satellites. It also produced a better-performing direct methanol oxidation fuel cell. What's that to you? Those fuel cells power your cars, boats, cell phones, and laptops.[22]

One of the best ways for governments to catalyze digitally disruptive innovations is through prizes and challenges, the subject we turn to next.

OPENING UP: REWARDING RESULTS THROUGH THE POWER OF PRIZES

Philadelphia has long had a crime problem. In 2014, the City of Brotherly Love was ranked the seventh-most dangerous big city in the country.[23] Unfortunately, that wasn't an aberration: Philadelphia has been one of the country's more dangerous cities throughout the last decade.

In 2014, Mayor Michael Nutter decided to try a different approach to cutting crime: launching a competition. The city crafted a $100,000 challenge called FastFWD and invited entrepreneurs to develop innovative solutions to crime. "We wanted to open up the solution space," explains Story Bellows, who led the initiative for the city. "We were looking for solutions we didn't expect and didn't even know existed."

In addition to $10,000 in seed money, each of the winners earned the chance to do a pilot project with the city. One of the winners was Jail Education Solutions, a tablet-based learning platform built for inmates by a young entrepreneur whose father was an educator at California's Folsom State Prison. "We know that educational training reduces recidivism and saves taxpayer dollars, so we're excited that Philadelphia is enabling technology that can improve the opportunities of so many returning to our communities," says Jail Education cofounder Brian Hill.[24]

The city of Philadelphia is just one of many jurisdictions turning to incentive prizes to try to solve thorny problems. Challenges are becoming an increasingly important tool for societal problem solving. They unite problems with problem solvers, filling holes in business models that cater mostly to traditional buyer-seller relationships. Prize programs engage problem solvers who are often neglected by government's traditional procurement and research grant systems. "What prizes allow you to do is reach beyond the people that are on government contract schedules, the people that are traditionally the folks that are responding to these kinds of things," explains Jenn Gustetic, the assistant director for open innovation at the White House.[25]

Furthermore, contests promote the commingling of ideas in a way that isolated, closed-door research and development efforts can't. In the Philadelphia case, as part of the selection criteria, city officials looked for startups with complementary skills that could collaborate with each other after being chosen.

Prize programs also offer a cost-effective alternative to traditional government procurements. The procurement process funds approaches, whereas prizes reward results. And while the procurement system favors players with traditional credentials and proven track records, competitions accept anyone, thereby multiplying the number and diversity of brains tackling a problem.

These represent just a few of the reasons why government leaders are increasingly turning to challenges to find innovative solutions to problems. Challenges can help policymakers do everything from attracting new ideas to stimulating markets to mobilizing action.[26]

Governments already have a good bit of experience running effective, high-impact prize challenges. For example, New York City's Big Apps competition released city data to participants, incentivizing them to develop mobile application solutions that use municipal data to solve citywide problems. The winners of the

2013 contest included apps to identify healthy options at nearby restaurants, help parents find quality child care, calculate home-owners' savings from a range of solar power options, and teach kids software coding.

For governments wanting to get into the prize game, there is no need to reinvent the wheel. Hundreds of public sector prize competitions have been conducted over the past half decade, more than 440 at the federal level alone. Gustetic, the former leader of NASA's prize and challenges program, has been involved in designing and overseeing dozens of government prizes and challenges. In the last decade, she has seen a quantum leap in the number and sophistication of these competitions as an alternative to traditional procurement. "We have 600 people in the federal government who have run to some extent or been involved in a prize or challenge," she says. "We've moved from the innovators phase to the early adopters phase, which is where you see the most interesting experimentation."

Policymakers can leverage the best practices from these efforts to avoid some of the early hiccups when designing their own challenges and prizes. These principles can help:

- **Design prizes after clearly defining the problem and specifying the desired outcome.** Successful public sector prize designers carefully study the problem area they are hoping to address and determine exactly what they want to achieve through the use of a prize.
- **Use prizes when there isn't a clear, defined approach to solving a problem.** Prizes are particularly effective in inspiring creativity and novel approaches. Competitions work best when a large number of diverse participants

can approach the problem in a variety of ways. "One of the questions that we ask when thinking about launching a prize is, does it exist in the marketplace or could it be developed in the marketplace by known actors?" explains Gustetic. If the answer is no, it's full steam ahead.

- **Use prizes to help fix customer delivery and citizen support issues.** "Digital government teams get a view into a lot of the customer issues agencies are facing," explains Gustetic. "In addition to using agile development tools, tapping into external communities for solutions could help to fix some of the issues. They can address community behavior, user experience, hardware, all sorts of things."

- **Create scenarios where all competitors—not only the winners—will emerge with something valuable.** Whether it is mentorship during solution development, networking opportunities with potential investors, or elevating public awareness of an issue, it is important for all individuals and teams to feel that they have gotten something out of their participation.

- **Use prizes as a force multiplier.** Prizes can improve the creative capacity of a government or organization by several orders of magnitude when they crowdsource the answers to questions at the edge of an industry. Prize mechanisms that are properly designed create relationships between participants, fostering a sense of competition and community that inspires them to invest more time, energy, and financial resources into developing a solution than they would in a more traditional context. For example, the MIT Clean Energy

Prize, sponsored by the Department of Energy, sought to spur the development of clean energy technology. With $1 million and some additional administration costs, the designers were able to incentivize teams to develop business plans that generated $85 million in capital and research grants.

Incentive prizes are powerful tools of digital change. They build and maintain communities of interest that help governments address complex, ambiguous problems. Prizes also create opportunities for public organizations to share costs with private and philanthropic partners. They foster collaboration among government, academia, the private sector, and individuals. These partners can help cover various costs associated with the prize, including providing the actual incentive, venue, administration, outreach to the targeted communities, and general marketing.

Most important, prizes and challenges show that government can innovate in the service of the public good and open up problem solving to take advantage of previously untapped ingenuity. Can the prize and challenge model itself be used to solve one of the biggest obstacles to digital-age procurement, namely a dearth of people in government who know how to contract for agile development and other innovative approaches?

TRAINING GOVERNMENT BUYERS IN DIGITAL-AGE ACQUISITION

The commercial world has been using agile, modular development and similar digital-friendly approaches for years. One side effect is that there are plenty of people in the private sector with experience buying these services—but not so in government.

Most government acquisition workforces have little to no experience contracting for digital services developed using an agile approach. In our global survey of 1,200 government officials, three out of four respondents said that procurement must change to accommodate digital transformation, especially to allow for agile development and less restrictive terms and conditions.[27] They identified regulations, lack of flexibility, and lack of procurement skill sets as the most significant obstacles to digital-friendly procurement.

One approach to solving the procurement skills issue would be to take a page out of the UK and US Digital Services book and recruit a bunch of private sector procurement people with cutting-edge skills in buying digital services. While this sounds reasonable, in reality it won't work in this area because it takes years to learn all the ins and outs of government procurement, making it impractical to bring in outsiders on short-term assignments.

Enter Traci Walker and Joanie Newhart, two federal procurement veterans, now with the US Digital Service and Office of Federal Procurement Policy, respectively, with a vision for solving the problem. Their idea was simple: to train and develop an elite cadre of digital contracting officers within the existing acquisition community, who would be the go-to people for buying digital services in government.

While a straightforward idea, the challenge was how to get there. These procurement officials would have to be trained in the new digital skill sets, but such a training program did not yet exist. "There are all kinds of training for the acquisition workforce in federal regulations, but little in the way of best IT and digital service practices, like agile," explains Walker, a federal contracting officer with 15 years of experience.[28] They would have to start from scratch.

The traditional approach to creating such a training problem would be to spend months and months gathering requirements and then put out an RFP to the market to develop an agile contracting training program. Walker and Newhart categorically rejected this course of action. Instead, "we decided to eat our own dog food," says Walker.

By that, she meant the pair looked at guidance to other agencies given by the US Digital Service at improving the speed and efficiency of digital government, and adapted it to their own project. "We didn't know what we wanted for the training," says Newhart. "But industry knows how to do this, so we took a page from the US Digital Service and did a phased approach."

They started with a "Reverse Industry Day" where, instead of telling industry about the federal government's requirements, they spent the day listening to companies talk about their ideas and experiences in this area. "We said to them, 'We want to hear what you've done, and what are your ideas,'" says Newhart.

From there they posted a call on Challenge.gov for a training program that could produce a new generation of government digital service procurement experts in six months or less. The objectives were clear: At the end of the program, the trainees would need to "understand and apply strategic thinking, industry best practices, marketplace conditions, and appropriate acquisition strategies to the procurement of digital supplies and services." They would need to be flexible, adaptive, focused on innovation, and able to judge the success of a contract based on industry standards.

The challenge itself proceeded in phases: technical concepts from all, detailed design and demonstration projects from three finalists, and execution of a pilot training program by the winner with 30 federal contracting officers as the participants. To encourage entries, the sponsors said participants would be eligible for up to $360,000 in prize money. "We're trying to create a marketplace where more and more vendors will offer this kind of training in agile contracting in government," says Newhart.

Following the pilot, the training participants will receive the first-ever Digital Service Contracting Officer Certification, which will identify them as subject matter experts. This will allow them the ability to work with agency digital service teams on digital services procurements and as champions for adopting the new, agile procurement approaches they learn.

NEW MINDSETS

At a conference Naggar organized in 2015 for innovative acquisition, Anne Rung, administrator of the Office of Federal Procurement Policy, remarked that one of the key obstacles to procurement innovation is the mindset in government that failure is not an option. "We don't tolerate any kind of perceived failure. And people immediately walk away and resort to the old way of doing things."[29]

It's ironic and telling that a culture this intolerant of failure is so prone to it. The private sector realized long ago that it's better to make a lot of little mistakes that help you get the big stuff right, instead of the other way around. Maybe they're on to something? After all, just about every tech giant you can name subscribes to the idea of "fail fast, fail often."

So perhaps it is time for this kind of mentality in government IT procurement. And there is no doubt people want to try something new. The fact that nearly 600 federal employees from 20 different agencies attended Naggar's conference is testament to that.[30]

The question is whether the culture of government can truly embrace these risks, and the people who take them, knowing that they are essential to make change.

BUILDING BETTER AVENUES TO PROCURE DIGITAL SERVICES

SUCCESS STRATEGIES

Consult early—and often. Amending the request-for-proposal (RFP) process to encourage early engagement and discussions with vendors would help give them a better idea of what an agency is looking for—not to mention encouraging a greater diversity of solutions. Consulting early with vendors can also help government officials ensure that what they are asking for is clear and that they are asking for the best technologies to address their needs.

First tell, then show how it works. Break out the procurement process into a two-stage downselect process. In the first stage, ask for a short concept paper and cost proposal (roughly six to eight pages). After selecting a handful of finalists, ask for a more detailed cost proposal and performance work statement—as well as a functioning prototype.

Conceptualize, propose, and pilot. Another variant of a two-stage downselect is staged contracts. They consist of three stages, starting with a short concept paper, then an invite-only full proposal, and finally a pilot evaluation. This lets evaluators get hands-on and see which contractor really understands their needs.

Show me the prototype. Rather than sink a bunch of dollars into every new technology that comes along, issue contracts for a number of small, inexpensive prototypes that can be built and evaluated quickly. This allows you to test the viability of new and unproven—but potentially transformative—technologies without risking too many taxpayer dollars.

Convert contracts into competitions. In milestone-based competitions, procurement officers carve up projects into smaller, technically feasible targets that are then opened up for competition to a pool of selected contractors. But flipping the payment model a bit, withhold payment until each agreed-upon milestone is "won," and milestones are released gradually until a project is complete. Since each milestone is independent of the others, this helps government agencies maintain flexibility and limit risk.

Make IT procurement an attractive career choice. Elevate the status of IT procurement as a career path within government. To get the best and the brightest into the profession, offer the same advancement and recognition potential as other career paths, especially ones that are perceived as more "mission oriented."

Train procurement officers in digital acquisition. Often, the government has a one-size-fits-all approach to procurement. But the first step is to realize that digital transformation requires a new set of procurement rules. Recruiting procurement talent well versed with agile and other cutting-edge methods is not always feasible. Instead, focus on training acquisition officers to be flexible, adaptive, and innovative when it comes to digital procurement.

Tap into private sector expertise. Although agile contracting is a bit new to governments, the private sector uses it extensively. Tap into that expertise. Partnerships and industry days offer a few ways that government procurement executives can spend time with private sector counterparts to learn new procurement techniques.

TOOLS AND TECHNIQUES

Bake-offs. An alternative to big multiyear awards, these are smaller awards to teams from different contractors. Every six months, they are reevaluated and the number of teams from each contractor is adjusted based on performance. Since the teams will have to work together, evaluate them not just on their own performance but on how well they collaborate.

Prizes and challenges. These can be quite effective at helping you engage a diverse, and often unexpected, group of problem solvers. Better yet, you pay only for results. But ensure that there are incentives for all competitors rather than just the winners. Incentives could be in the form of learning from other participants or building a network of like-minded innovators.

RESOURCES (WEBSITES, BOOKS, AND OTHER COOL STUFF)

One of the digital plays from the US Digital Services Playbook discusses how to structure budgets and contracts to support delivery. It has a checklist that procurement officers and agency leaders can follow. [https://playbook.cio.gov/#play5]

"Open" is one of the basic tenets of digital transformation. Why should procurement be any different? The Open Contracting Data Standard project aims to evolve a process through which contracting data and documents can be published in an accessible, structured, and repeatable way. [http://ocds.open-contracting.org/standard/r/1__0__RC/en/standard/intro/]

As part of the What Works Cities initiative, the Government Performance Lab provides technical assistance to governments that seek to adopt result-driven contracting strategies for their critical grants and procurements. [http://govlab.hks.harvard.edu/]

The HHS Buyers Club strategy document is freely available on the web. If you are looking to start something similar at your agency, the strategy document is a good starting point. [www.hhs.gov/idealab/wp-content/uploads/2014/11/HHS-Buyers-Club-Strategy-11-5-2014.pdf]

All US federal employees can join a federal-wide buyers club list to receive regular updates in the area. You can register for the listserv on the GSA website. [https://listserv.gsa.gov/cgi-bin/wa.exe?SUBED1=BUYERS-CLUB&A=1]

The US Digital Services Playbook includes the TechFAR handbook, which provides a series of best practices for agencies looking to procure digital services using agile processes. [https://goo.gl/eNhVKT]

How to Fix Procurement by Clay Johnson, a former director at the Sunlight Foundation, outlines seven "fixes" for government technology procurement. The short book is free and available on GitHub. [http://goo.gl/CMH2jT]

CHAPTER 5

HACKING THE SILOS:
Horizontal Government

EATING THE ELEPHANT

For a little light reading, consider a tome released by the US Office of Management and Budget on January 29, 2013, *Federal Enterprise Architecture Framework: Version 2.*[1] It's a 434-page roadmap addressing perhaps the most vexing IT problem facing federal government: how to identify thousands of redundant and overlapping computer systems and databases across agencies and consolidate them into enterprise systems that any department can use.

Under an enterprise system, departments of education and transportation, for instance, would use the same payroll system. Personnel administration, grants, benefits administration, acquisitions, and finance could all be streamlined in this way. The practical benefits would be enormous.

Despite the scale and importance of this challenge, the record of attempts thus far is a litany of failure. It began in 1996, with the passage of the Clinger-Cohen Act, which requires all federal chief information officers to develop, maintain, and facilitate integrated systems. The aim of the act was laudable, of course. The problem was that it completely ignored certain fundamental realities of the federal bureaucracy. As Paul Strassmann, a well-respected IT blogger, writes:

> At present CIOs cannot be held accountable for the contracting decisions that are made by acquisition officers who use regulations found on 2,017 pages printed in small font. The management of IT, as of March 2011, is split into 2,258 business systems...[2]

As of late 2015, the situation hadn't changed much. It's codified chaos.

That doesn't mean that people haven't *tried* to change it. Among the veterans is Mark Forman, named by President George W. Bush as the first "e-government czar" in American history. Forman's instructions to federal agencies were straightforward:

> Use commodity instead of proprietary hardware and software. Move... to shared resources where agencies build for component reuse and integration. Stop building monolithic applications and apply the shared service approach. Automate more IT services to improve their quality.[3]

The initiative had a few genuine successes—26 payroll systems were consolidated, and e-travel services were consolidated with four providers—but ultimately fell far short of its ambitious goals.

"The Bush administration tried," says Tony Summerlin, chief data officer at the Federal Communications Commission (FCC) and then part of Forman's team. He recalled White House chief of staff Josh Bolton and Office of Management and Budget (OMB) director Mitch Daniels yelling, "You're gonna do this!" at meetings with deputy cabinet secretaries.[4] The president himself attended occasional meetings, Summerlin says, and tried to turn up the heat on participants if he wasn't seeing adequate progress.

Forman and Summerlin attribute failure to the usual causes: federal fiefdoms run by people more interested in consolidating power than sharing information; agencies too completely consumed by day-to-day operations to focus on IT integration; fundamental ignorance of IT integration and its implications at the staff level; the fear of losing control over data security; budgeting that encourages silos; and the fundamentally flawed approach to contracting described in chapter 4.

Perhaps paradoxically, however, what really blocked the effort was its ambition. "We tried 'rip and replace,'" Forman explains. "But it's very, very difficult to totally wean yourself off legacy applications that built up over 30 years."[5] Or, as Summerlin colorfully puts it: "You have to eat the elephant with a spoon. You can't go after it with a jackhammer. You'll lose every time with an all-or-nothing approach."

The first, simple spoonful is asking what an ideal, integrated government might look like.

THE CASE FOR A HORIZONTALLY INTEGRATED GOVERNMENT

In his 2008 book *The Next Government of the United States: Why Our Institutions Fail Us and How to Fix Them*, political scientist Donald Kettl introduced the concept of an antiquated "vending machine" style of government that provides standalone services such as education, health care, and tax collections.[6] Vending-machine governments are hierarchical, operating in vertical silos. This structure works well for routine services that don't require collaboration across departmental boundaries. But it falters when we need highly networked government—which is most of the time.

Nowhere would the advantages of connected government be more visible than in the way departments interact with citizens and businesses. Imagine never having to retype your address on another sign-up form. If departments used the same systems and shared data with one another, many annoying and time-consuming repetitive tasks would vanish: With a single digital identifier to authenticate themselves, for instance, citizens would be able to go online and pay taxes, arrange health care coverage, apply for small business loans, register a corporation, vote in national elections, and sign legally binding documents without retyping the same information over and over again. Interaction with government would become quick and efficient.

Inside government, duplication and overlap in IT systems would become obsolete. Ten different agencies that each had their own payroll applications, for instance, could shift to a single payroll system that could be customized as needed.

What would be the key features of an optimized "enterprise" model of government? Common processes and capabilities—data analytics, web hosting, publishing, email, identity management—would become the basic building blocks. Shared capabilities would become common, while custom applications would be minimized.[7] The goal would be a seamless, or "horizontal" government offering lower costs and improved performance.

COSTS

Between 2008 and 2013, the US Government Accountability Office (GAO) found IT projects in just three departments—Defense, Homeland Security, and Health and Human Services—had spent more than $321 million to duplicate the efforts of other projects within the same departments.[8] Even more significant opportunities for savings exist *across* agencies. Whenever multiple agencies carry out common processes—payments, payroll, authentication, reservations—they can save considerable amounts of money by sharing systems.

Britain's former digital chief Mike Bracken explains: "There isn't one IT system in government, not a single one, that has managed to service the needs of all the other government departments. So the definition of platform would be that it's additive—it services everyone, and every new user adds value."[9]

Rough estimates suggest that a platform approach to government services could save the United Kingdom £35 billion each year.[10] According to the government, its publishing platform Gov.uk has already consolidated 300 websites and saved taxpayers £60 million.[11]

PERFORMANCE

For years, Indiana's infant mortality had been troublingly high, despite a number of state initiatives to improve matters. The problem? "When you don't have the data, you go with your gut," says Chris Atkins, Indiana's former Office of Management and

Budget director. "People thought the key levers were smoking, drug use, et cetera—all of which turned out to be wrong."[12]

Under Atkins's leadership, Indiana's OMB team discovered that a certain group of mothers accounted for just 1.6 percent of births but almost *half* of all infant deaths and 35 percent of Medicaid's birth-related expenses. The data revealed these women, while enrolled in Medicaid, were not getting the recommended number of prenatal visits. Further analysis found that one reason was simply a lack of transportation. "We were like, wow, it's just a matter of getting the mother to the appointment," says Indiana's former CIO Paul Baltzell.[13] The state then identified ways to connect expectant mothers with affordable public transit.

Mind you, it took work to wring these conclusions from the data. Groundwork for the project involved tracking down and "cleaning" multiple data sets. OMB's analysts studied 17 integrated data sets from multiple agencies and public sources, including demographic and health data, financial information, and criminal histories, all mapped by location.[14] Their findings were so useful that the state plans to extend their analytical techniques to areas such as recidivism and child protection.

A FOUNDATION FOR DIGITAL GOVERNMENT

As Indiana's experience shows, horizontal government can illuminate problems and improve performance. It also lays a good foundation for the broader digital transformation of government.

If we go back to the tenets of digital government—simple, open, agile, and user-centric—it's evident that the platform approach supports all of them. Giant, monolithic, single-purpose systems don't. "If you want to change radically," Bracken says, "you first need to redesign your institutional model."

Digital transformation is as much about organizational culture as it is about technology. A horizontal model punches holes through agency silos, improving efficiency and reinforcing a culture of openness and sharing. Its digital tools are built on data sharing and uniform standards.[15]

This vision of horizontal government is hardly new. For nearly two decades, public-sector consultants have been presenting beautiful PowerPoint depictions of technology operating seamlessly across organizational silos. Horizontal government looks great on screen, but agencies have struggled to achieve it.

Nevertheless, governments from New York City to Tallinn are making progress, employing innovative approaches to overcome institutional barriers concerning systems, data, and identity management.

PLUG-AND-PLAY: TACKLING DUPLICATION AND OVERLAP

"I often say I feel like Oprah Winfrey," says David Bray, who became CIO of the FCC in late 2013.[16] "Everyone look under your chair: You're getting your own legacy system today!"[17]

For many years, that's just how the FCC was run. "When I arrived, we had at least 207 different IT systems for 1,750 civil servants," Bray says. "Every time a new effort was requested by Congress or the administration, they just created a new system. At a certain point, that's just unsustainable."[18]

It wasn't just the number of systems—nearly one for every nine employees—that caught Bray's attention. Many of them were terribly outdated. Bray found data centers lacking anything remotely resembling modern heating, ventilation, and cooling systems. Much of the software hadn't been touched since the 1990s. And the worst part for an administrator looking to make big changes: Nearly 80 percent of his operating budget was allocated to keep all of it running.[19]

In a very public scene in 2014, the FCC saw an unprecedented and dramatic surge in online comments as millions of people, inspired by HBO host John Oliver's rant on net neutrality, tried to post—and found the system buckling under the onslaught.[20] By then, Bray was already well aware that the agency needed to replace its aging technology.

As he saw it, the FCC had two choices. One was to try to modernize each of the 207 different systems. "But by the time we finished doing that, we probably would have had to do it all over again," he says. The alternative was to shift the agency's IT systems from application-centric to *data-centric*—in other words, use commercial cloud platforms to create a common virtual repository for FCC data serving all the agency's functions. This would ease the transition to newer technology and provide some much-needed flexibility.

This approach was cheaper and fit the FCC's constraints much better. "We have to respond to directions from Congress, which can require us to change on a dime," Bray says. "So the idea was, let's have a single common data platform that has all the data from the legacy systems, and over time use modular elements of commercial cloud platforms to deliver reusable, remixable processes for the FCC."[21]

Bray's data-centric approach focused on the steps each process would use to interact with the common data. "While each process is different, as with issuing or updating a license, they probably follow similar steps in terms of first needing to authenticate who you are," he says. "Maybe along the way I want to ask for some data. Maybe I actually want to produce a file so they can have a receipt."[22]

Bray's team used modular pieces of code that can be used and reused to interact with the common data platform. These modules are like pieces of yarn that can be woven together in infinite ways to match the needs of each process or new demand from Congress.

It's a governmental variation on the plug-and-play model adapted for the cloud computing age. Instead of building big, heavy applications that commingle code and data, the agency chose to develop smaller, lightweight modules of code that drink from a more permanent "data lake." By separating data and code, Bray realized, the FCC could more easily "remix" the code to meet congressional demands. The system would cost far less to maintain while making the agency much more nimble and responsive.

Think of it as cake baking. You don't know which customers will come into your bakery. Instead of adding nuts and fruit to the cake batter, why not bake a plain cake and add toppings later? Then you can replace almonds with walnuts, or nuts with fruit, for little or no additional cost. That's how the plug-and-play model can work for government: It shares the essential ingredients (data) and customizes the flourishes (the code).

To undertake this transformation, Bray led the FCC through what he terms a "lift and shift," essentially a way to migrate IT systems while keeping them online and functioning through the transition. Leading up to this, some legacy systems are retired, others consolidated or moved to newer hardware to keep them alive, and some moved directly to a public cloud. In the first phase, the "lift," you transfer the agency's current systems to an offsite commercial managed-services provider. Then you determine what systems you want to keep, cut, or move to the cloud. Finally, there's the actual migration, the "shift."

At the FCC, Bray put all 207 systems on the chopping block. Mary Ellen Seale, a member of his team, says multiple offices then worked together to decide, "Should we keep this, divest it, modernize it, move to a different version, or completely reengineer it?"

They weren't afraid to make cuts. After only six months, Bray's team had eliminated 113 systems before the server lift, bringing the total down to 94. For those the team chose to modernize, off-the-shelf cloud solutions generally worked fine, such as Microsoft Office 365's public cloud and ZenDesk, an online cloud-based customer service suite. Bray was insistent on getting the FCC out of the business of building and managing its own IT. Now, the agency considers writing code only after all other avenues are exhausted.

By the middle of 2015, the strategy was delivering results. The agency's move to ZenDesk was particularly successful, Bray says. It reduced a process for filing consumer complaints that involved 18 forms to a single, TurboTax–style web page that's much, *much* easier for users—and far less expensive than a custom solution. Bray estimates the agency saved about $500,000 on software by using off-the-shelf products and another $3 million by not building the related infrastructure.[23]

Moving to the cloud, Bray says, is "a value proposition" for the public and Capitol Hill, providing better security than agency-built solutions and giving the FCC the agility it needs to create cost-effective new systems in response to demands from the administration or Congress.[24]

Needless to say, the transformation wasn't without challenges—as with any major transition, you can't always get everyone affected to sign on, and sometimes they have good reasons. But the FCC provides an example of how to minimize such complications by working with and within agency culture.

For the FCC, Bray says, "It was 20 percent technology, 80 percent people. A lot of people approach IT transformation as 80 percent technology and 20 percent people—and that's what screws things up." If you focus on empowering people to be positive "change agents" at all levels, he explains, then you begin to shift behaviors as well as technologies, until they become habits and ultimately transform an organization's way of working.[25]

Over Labor Day weekend in 2015, Bray and his team completed the lift of all their servers to a managed service provider. This means that all of FCC's systems, once run in-house, are now either in a public, commercial cloud or hosted by a commercial server provider as a cloud service.

LEARNING FROM THE FCC

The FCC's modernization initiative offers several important lessons for governments planning to share IT services.

First, pioneering the horizontal model at a department level, or within a specific line of business such as human services or revenue and taxation, is a good way to start. It's usually less complex than a government-wide effort and easier to get people on board. Moreover, as the FCC demonstrates, there's usually abundant room for consolidation and reuse. A successful transformation effort then becomes a de facto proof of concept, dispelling doubts among those who'll use the new model—and those who finance it. A trial can help garner support by previewing a positive outcome before large-scale investment.

Second, it's critical to go through a rigorous discovery process to identify silos and build a repository of common systems, processes, and capabilities.[26] It's akin to dismantling an auto engine in a mechanics class. Where does each part go? What does it do? How does everything work together as a system?

Bray rightly spent a lot of time on the discovery phase, profiling each of the FCC's 207 systems to separate common capabilities from custom applications. His team combed the systems with an audit including cyberhygiene, vulnerability assessment, and a full hardware inventory.[27] It helped differentiate between hopeless systems and those that could be improved. "Don't assume it's broken," Bray says.

Finally, the FCC's decision to focus on data rather than applications paid off. Applications are replaceable; data may not be. Consider the byzantine consumer complaint process FCC revamped: The agency was, rather incredibly, sending 18 separate forms to each complainant, leaving them to decide which to complete. FCC flipped the model by focusing on customers' needs. Today, the ZenDesk-based system generates the appropriate form based on input from the complaining customer.

BRANCHING OUT: CREATING SYSTEMS BUILT AROUND DATA EXCHANGES

Ultimately, governments will want to expand the plug-and-play model across departments, agencies, and lines of business. As they do so, they'll need to answer a number of key questions: Which areas should they tackle first? What approach should they undertake? And how can they fund it?

For an initial foray into building common, reusable platforms, it's useful (as always) to start small and shoot for a quick win. This was clearly the strategy of the 18F team behind the September 2015 launch of the White House Social and Behavioral Sciences Team website.[28] One more website in a plethora of dot-gov domains is hardly news. But this one was different. It was built using 18F's new Federalist publishing platform, a suite of tools that allows agencies to build their own secure, responsive, and accessible websites.

Federalist integrates several pre-existing platforms, including content editor GitHub, Amazon Web Services, and support for Microsoft's Azure. It's a first step toward a plug-and-play model that allows agencies to scale and reuse systems according to their needs.

In the United Kingdom, the Government Digital Service (GDS) had already built four such platforms by 2012, for publishing (Gov.uk), identity management (Verify), procurement (Digital Marketplace), and performance management. But this was just the start: "We have done it four times, but we think we need between 20 and 30 of those things," Mike Bracken said before he left government.[29]

Another good starter project would be a common technology infrastructure. The workforce deserves better everyday tools that allow employees to spend less time worrying about IT and more time on work. Consider the transformation effort at the UK Cabinet Office. The office faced a fairly typical collection of IT problems: poor Wi-Fi, inadequate Internet tools, outdated browsers, and time drag during the sign-on process. When their IT services contract ran out, cabinet officials decided to set up a new Digital and Technology Team to develop latest-generation web tools and cloud applications.[30] The effort was expanded government-wide. Its Common Technology Services Team centralizes IT services with cloud solutions, common design, common products, and reusable services.[31]

When it comes to what approach to use, it's wise to steer clear of the "rip and replace" model. Bray's big insight at the FCC was that in a world of cloud computing, open-source technology, software as a service, and ubiquitous API services (which help computers, websites, or applications interact at the back end), the data element, not the applications, is the key to creating horizontal IT systems that cut across silos. In this world, creating an enterprise system is often less about trying to corral dozens of disparate agencies into using a single platform and more about creating systems of systems built around data exchanges and with a common understanding of how that shared data is defined.

A good analogy would be smart energy grids. These next-generation electricity grids use digital processing, computer-based remote control, and automation to transport not only energy but also data-enabling end-user energy management in the form of smart meters, smart appliances, and energy efficiency resources. Critical to making smart grids work is the digital layer, which enables the data flow necessary to make the applications smart, coupled with the use of a data standard to make these smart applications interact with each other and take advantage of the data being exchanged. Importantly, the data layer sits on top of the existing energy grid infrastructure, as opposed to replacing all the wires, substations, transformers, and switches that constitute the grid.

A system of data exchanges built on top of legacy IT systems would work in a similar fashion. A good example is the National Information Exchange Model (NIEM) created after the September

11, 2001, attacks to facilitate information sharing among law enforcement and homeland security organizations.

NIEM started out as an initiative of the US Department of Justice (DOJ) but morphed into a joint approach when the Department of Homeland Security (DHS) and then later the Department of Health and Human Services (HHS) came on board. It's in essence a coordinated protocol for sharing information between normally siloed departments both during emergencies and on a day-to-day basis.

"No one was really sharing information between them, even within the federal law enforcement community," explains Van Hitch, the DOJ's onetime CIO who founded NIEM. "In the past, the primary way to share information was to set up a task force with members from all relevant agencies."

The lack of means to share information was on full display with the 2002 Beltway sniper attacks, in which 10 people were killed and several others were critically injured in locations throughout the Washington, DC, metropolitan area. The two shooters had started their crime spree months earlier with multiple murders and robberies in seven other states, but the lack of law enforcement information sharing across states meant that each shooting was treated as a localized incident instead of the nationwide shooting rampage that was actually occurring. With real-time information sharing between police departments, the shooters might have been apprehended much sooner.

NIEM was built to prevent this kind of situation from happening again. At its core is a governance protocol that sets some standard definitions for key data fields—"person," "location," "activity," "item," and so forth—as well as for message types that can be adopted across disparate jurisdictions and departments, allowing for rapid, widespread access to and sharing of information. It's like a data dictionary with thousands of data fields and individual chapters specific to sectors using NIEM such as justice, transportation, homeland security, and social services.

Getting NIEM off the ground required a lot more than just the technology. Hitch had to sell the idea to dozens of key stakeholders. "Standards like NIEM have a network effect," he explains. "The more people who use them, the more data exchanges that are built off them, the better and more valuable they become." For NIEM to be successful, Hitch needed to convince dozens of state, local, and federal law enforcement agencies to adopt the standard. "Getting alliances was critical," he says. "There were already groups that were set up to help bring law enforcement together. I really cultivated those groups—went to all of their national conferences and got law enforcement on board at least from an aspiration standpoint."

Hitch also had to secure funding for NIEM, a notoriously difficult task for a horizontal government initiative, since funding tends to flow from legislative committees into individual departments. Rather than trying to get a line item in DOJ's budget, he convinced DOJ and DHS to each contribute via a combination of grants and direct funding, so each would have some skin in the game. Over the years, the NIEM Program Management Office has made it a priority to continue to find new partners.

As of January 2016, all 50 states, at least 16 federal agencies, and even many foreign governments have adopted the NIEM standard. NIEM has, for example, helped to better secure the border between Canada and the United States. For many years, the two countries lacked a coordinated way to share information on border crossings—a person entering one country was not necessarily identified as having left the other country. So the two countries worked together to develop the Entry/Exit program, in which confirmed entry into one country is considered exit from the other, helping officials track persons of interest and ultimately increasing public safety and security.

NIEM enabled Canada and the United States to avoid the headache of trying to build an integrated system together—instead, engineers used the program to connect the countries' legacy systems through a common approach to data sharing. NIEM already contained the terms and definitions required for the exchange; these were reused, allowing the IT teams to quickly define the structure of the exchange. As a result, NIEM-based transactions now flow between the two countries 365 days a year.

Besides its obvious utility in the national security arena, NIEM has matured to the point where numerous state and local jurisdictions have also adopted the standard to coordinate information and action in a wide variety of areas, from law enforcement to human services. For example, Massachusetts uses NIEM to share information related to gangs and gang activity among a wide variety of state and local law enforcement agencies. New York City, meanwhile, uses the program to allow residents to sign up for social service programs using a single portal. And child welfare agencies have created an information exchange built off NIEM to speed the arduously slow process of placing children across state lines. The exchange, which allows disparate child welfare data systems to exchange information on children, has slashed the approval time from 6–12 months to 1–2 days.

Whatever approach to integration is chosen, one key barrier inevitably arises: how to finance a horizontal government model. Currently, IT funding often flows to individual departments and agencies, leaving little for broader cross-government initiatives.

To encourage horizontal growth, governments should target funds to the players most critical to digital progress. Instead of allocating funds to individual agencies, for instance, money could be directed to an overhead group, such as 18F or the UK's GDS, which can provide infrastructure to *all* agencies, essentially functioning as a back end to government.

FLOWERS'S GEEK SQUAD

In 2011, New York City found itself in a literally sticky situation: Its sewers were clogged with oil and grease because some restaurants were illegally dumping the contents of deep fryers and pans straight into the drain. The resulting backups and messes were cringe-worthy and expensive; just clearing backups was costing the city nearly $5 million a year.[32]

How did the city identify the guilty parties? With an unlikely squad of number crunchers.

The city's Office of Policy and Strategic Planning (later called the Mayor's Office of Data Analytics), a crew of geeky problem solvers, combined geospatial analytics and public data on restaurants' waste disposal processes to track down suspects. The data crunchers boiled down their analysis to a single map that led the Department of Environmental Protection straight to the kitchens of rogue restaurants with striking accuracy—95 percent of restaurants inspected proved to be illegal dumpers. The city then launched an educational drive aimed at the offenders. Instead of levying $25,000 fines, it provided them with a list of registered biodiesel companies that could dispose of their kitchen waste.[33]

Led by Michael Flowers, New York's first chief analytics officer, the team went on to tackle a barrage of complex city problems, from illegal building conversions to the distribution of prescription drugs, by tapping data from siloed programs and combining them in different ways.

"I think of us as the Get Stuff Done Folks," Flowers told the *New York Times*. "All we do is take and process massive amounts of information and use it to do things more effectively."[34] Their goal was to show that city agencies could be far more effective by sharing their data than keeping it to themselves.[35]

Flowers became enamored of data analytics during a stint in Iraq. While investigating Saddam Hussein's government for the Justice Department, he saw military officers use predictive analytics to determine where bombs were likely to be set. He later applied similar data-driven techniques to a task force on mortgage fraud in New York City during the early years of the Great Recession.

Flowers's geek squad wasn't the city's first experience with data-driven decision making. CompStat, the police department's legendary criminal data system, was already two decades old, enabling officers to track crime and compare performance statistics among precincts and react quickly to changing situations.

But the data-driven approach was used primarily in individual departments and seldom deployed *across* government agencies to tackle problems such as youth employment or public health. What Flowers and other data-driven innovators have learned is that horizontal data sharing, often with the public as well as within government, can trigger major performance breakthroughs. "Our big insight was that data trapped in individual agencies should be liberated and used as an enterprise asset," Flowers explains.

By allowing disparate systems to share data, New York City's data layer became the conduit for interagency cooperation on cross-government issues. "Those agencies using it are now connected," says Flowers. The platform produces data-based insights that act as powerful incentives, pushing organizations to change processes that clearly aren't working. "You can't run from something that's glaring at you," he says. "You're going to be forced to confront it."[36]

With this philosophy in mind, one of Flowers's core goals was to liberate information whenever and wherever possible. "I just wanted to open the sluice gates," he says. "Let that information out, and good things are going to come from it. Now everybody's holding each other accountable where it was previously impossible."

One of the analytics squad's biggest breakthroughs came in the area of building inspections. Previously, the NYC Department of Buildings would inspect properties for unsafe conditions and structural hazards based largely on complaints received. In 2011, the city received almost 25,000 complaints about a single problem: illegal conversions. Landlords would divide apartments into smaller units to accommodate more people than the apartment was zoned for—or could safely house. Dozens of people might occupy a space meant for five, a potential disaster in terms of fire safety, crime, and public health.

With only 200 inspectors to investigate thousands of complaints, Flowers and his squad devised an analytical method to predict the most high-risk complaints. "When we prioritize the complaint list, we're reducing our time to respond to the most dangerous places, in effect reducing the number of days that residents are living at risk," Flowers says.[37]

Critically, the geek squad didn't create a fancy algorithm from their desks at City Hall—they built their predictive data model with the help of building inspectors who'd been in the field for years. "The field inspectors were like, 'Yeah, I know which places are dumps in this neighborhood, because I've been working this beat for so long,'" Flowers says. "So we injected that employee experience into the data and fed that into a risk filter." The result was a triaged list of properties for inspection.

The results were staggering. In previous follow-ups on complaints, only 13 percent ended up requiring vacate orders. Flowers's team dramatically reduced the number of false positives. The share of complaints leading to vacate orders escalated to *70 percent*.[38] "We didn't reengineer anything," Flowers says. "All we did was inject transparency into the process."[39]

He emphasizes that data can create transparency and accountability, describing it as "sunlight burning bad things." It can also produce unexpected revelations. Flowers discovered, for instance, that improved building inspections lowers risks for firefighters, since fires in illegal conversions were 15 times more likely than other fires to result in injury or death for firefighters.[40] "It's very, very clear that if the buildings department doesn't do its job, it's felt downstream by the fire department," he explains.[41]

Thanks in no small part to this analytics-driven approach, in June 2015, New York City experienced no fire deaths for the first time since 1916.[42]

The NYC building inspection story is a powerful reminder that shared data can help decision makers see connections and minutiae they might otherwise miss. This ability to connect data across government can literally mean the difference between life and death.

EXTENDING THE DATA LAYER

Ideally, the data layer encompasses not just agencies but citizens and other organizations, through open-government data initiatives. Open data allow ordinary citizens, nonprofits, corporations, and governments to build apps and tools and apply analytics to solve public problems.

Consider how New Orleans has used a combination of internal and open data to address fire fatalities. Since 2010, the city experienced 22 fire-related deaths. In 2014, one house fire killed five occupants, including three children. One contributing factor in almost all these fires was the absence of a smoke alarm.

New Orleans decided to use data science to formulate a preventive approach to firefighting. As part of its Targeted Smoke Alarm Outreach Program, the city developed a predictive model to identify areas at the highest risk of fires and fire fatalities. The data fed into the model came from open sources such as the Census American Housing Survey and American Community Survey, as well as the fire department's own data.

Taking into account factors such as poverty, building age, location, previous fire history, and the likelihood of dwellings having fire alarms, the project turned once-siloed data into actionable insights. Officials created a heat map of the city to pinpoint areas for a door-to-door campaign. For instance, since the analysis revealed that those under 5 and over 60 were most susceptible to fire fatalities, authorities distributed and installed fire alarms in areas with concentrations of these age groups.[43] New Orleans distributed more than 7,500 alarms by the end of 2015.[44] Analytics, cross-agency collaboration, and data integration helped the city optimize its resources to protect its most vulnerable residents.

Chicago authorities employ open data and analytics through the city's SmartData project. One of its first products was Windy-Grid, a geospatial web application consolidating Chicago's big data in a single location. Its offerings include video feeds from surveillance cameras, city transit location data, geospatially tagged 311 reports, 911 calls, public tweets, and emergency operations data. WindyGrid data can be used to produce insights at an unprecedented scale and speed: For instance, the system can analyze traffic and pedestrian patterns to predict and prevent collisions, or examine 311 call patterns to anticipate and prevent rodent outbreaks.

The platform's real potential lies in its ability to garner insights from formerly siloed data. The rodent situation provides a good example. Using garbage complaints as indicators, the city found that garbage complaints usually preceded a rodent complaint in the same spot within a few days.[45] Using analytics to link the two complaints, the city could kill two birds with one stone—or, rather, one service crew.

And Chicago shared its success. Its data infrastructure and algorithms are open-source; any city can reuse Chicago's architecture and tailor it to its specific data and needs. The city also offers templates and detailed documentation to guide municipalities in replicating the Chicago model.[46]

This integration of data from different sources in a single, unified data layer is essential to unlocking the true potential of government data and, thus, of digital government itself. The Estonian officials we met in the book's introduction understood the importance of the data layer very early on. They also realized that another key to truly digital government is a single, uniform identifier for every citizen and every business.

MANAGING IDENTITY

Imagine you were browsing Amazon.com for a few items: a book, a pair of shoes, and a new case for your iPhone. You log in and the experience is relatively smooth, but as soon as you find the book and move on to shoes, Amazon asks for your password again. Mildly annoyed, you re-enter it and carry on—until the same thing happens when you search for iPhone cases. And then *again* when it comes time to check out. By the time you've paid, you've had to authenticate yourself four times. And, weirdly, each time the process is just a little bit different. You find that you like the company just a little bit less.

Of course, that wouldn't happen on Amazon. But it's pretty familiar to anyone who uses online government services.

Governments rely on a sprawling patchwork of systems to identify and manage people, using everything from passwords to smart cards to biometrics. At the same time, the data must be tagged so that only the right users have access. Unfortunately, these elements rarely come together in a way that seems convenient or even logical to the end user, whether it's a citizen, a business, or even a government worker. Citizens can't file their taxes without reentering information several times; agency employees are locked out of buildings they should be able to enter because their radio-frequency identification (RFID) card is part of the West Coast system, while the East Coast offices use a different vendor. These disconnects can be frustrating at best and crippling at worst.

In the private sector, such hurdles are increasingly relics of the past, and their stubborn remnants in the public sector are sharply at odds with the idea of digital government. Whether you're working *in* or *with* government, you shouldn't have to authenticate your ID many times over, or re-enter data the government already has. Instead, the "customer experience" should be seamless, like Amazon's.

The problems stem from the way government manages identity: databases that can't talk with one another, limited information sharing, and overly complex rules and protocols. To make digital government work and deliver the customer experiences discussed in chapter 3, we need something simpler: a unique, uniform digital ID that grants agencies access to all of the appropriate data and services, from anywhere and any device.

Of course, this is far easier said than done. For a start, it raises enormous privacy issues; today's citizens often *fight* proposals for uniform digital IDs. In 2006, the British Parliament passed an act calling for national identity cards and a personal identification document. It was scrapped before implementation due to fierce public opposition.

Government digital IDs involve many other challenges as well, from technical and cultural silos to legacy systems and complex legal restrictions. And yet some countries *have* invested in uniform digital identity with success. Their experiences can provide a roadmap for governments navigating the earlier stages of the journey.

X-ROAD: ESTONIA'S UNIFORM DIGITAL IDENTIFIER

We start our tour of digital identity systems in Estonia, which as noted in the introduction probably has the world's most advanced digital government. How did that small country get there? After all, it emerged from 50 years of Soviet occupation only in 1991, with an infrastructure laid down in the 1930s.

But it turned out the timing was perfect: Estonia reclaimed its sovereignty at the dawn of the Internet age. Since the new nation was building many of its IT systems for the first time, the Internet played an outsized role. Nearly every aspect of Estonian government and business—taxes, banking, health care, you name it—was tailored for the online world. It's all linked by a data-exchange system called X-Road, which provides a highly robust model for digital identity.

The cornerstone of X-Road is the Estonian ID card, widely considered the most sophisticated of its kind. Estonian IDs serve both as physical documents, incorporating a photo and biometric data, and as digital identifiers. The card features an onboard chip containing two certificates, one for verifying identity and the other for digital signatures, each protected by a four-digit personal identification number (PIN). Every man, woman, and child in Estonia can provide strong identity authentication in person or at a distance. And since they can easily prove who they are, they can conduct business with the government or the private sector much more efficiently.

Transactions that in other countries require a trip to the bank or tax office and a briefcase bulging with documents can be conducted securely online. Using only their ID cards and PINs as credentials, Estonians can register a corporation, vote in national elections, and sign legally binding documents from their computers. It's seamless and efficient, and citizens are never asked for the same information twice. (In fact, Estonian law *prohibits* the government from making duplicative requests.)[47]

This identity system serves as the foundation for nearly all of Estonia's systems, public and private; citizens can connect to almost every digital service via X-Road. When Estonians fill out tax returns, for example, the government collates their data to help them. Charities already report donations, and banks already report mortgages—why should taxpayers have to resubmit that information? In Estonia, X-Road links and updates such information continuously throughout the year. For most Estonians, filing taxes amounts to clicking Next, Next, Next, Done.

It may smack of Big Brother, but a bedrock principle of the Estonian system is privacy. In fact, as the *Atlantic* has noted: "without question, it is always the [Estonian] citizen who owns his or her data and retains the right to control access to that data."[48] That's because X-Road isn't a centralized database but, rather, a highway, connecting a multitude of public and private databases—and citizens control the onramps.

Take Estonia's health system, for example. The platform is 100 percent digital: Everything from medical records to prescriptions is handled through the Internet. In many countries, you have no idea who has your medical data; in Estonia, you have complete control. A simple website lets you control access rights at a granular level, down to specific doctors of your choosing. And because medical professionals can only *see* the data, not store it, you can be sure that when you revoke a doctor's permission, he or she no longer has access to your records.

But what if you can't legally block someone from seeing your data, as with law enforcement? The system is still designed to protect privacy. Estonian officials have digital IDs, just like their constituents, and every time they access someone's data, X-Road logs it. This means that Estonians can visit a website and see which authorities have viewed their information and when. Notes the *Atlantic*, "If an honest citizen learns that an official has been snooping on them without a valid reason, the person can file an inquiry and get the official fired."[49]

With its identity platform, Estonia has managed to have the best of both worlds. The system can know everything about you when you want it to—and very little when you don't. And when the government needs full access, you have powerful tools to hold it accountable.

If it all seems a bit utopian, well, that's because it is. While the Estonian model is surely something to admire, the country owes much of its success to its unique history and demographics. Nearly everyone in government IT will tell you that one of their toughest challenges is dealing with legacy systems. Estonia didn't have to: Its IT teams could start from scratch with the most current technology. In addition, the country is small—only about 1.3 million people—making it significantly easier to design and implement digital government.

That said, Estonia's story highlights several challenges facing governments as they build uniform digital ID programs. Let's explore a number of these challenges and some ideas for overcoming them.

FOUR OBSTACLES TO UNIFORM DIGITAL ID

Digital identity management is a technological and political minefield. At some point, you may find yourself at odds with constituents, colleagues, or both. Inevitably, spies, hackers, and criminals will come raiding. Navigating the danger involves four key issues: data sharing, privacy, security, and public adoption.

DATA SHARING

Estonia's digital government program demonstrates the power of linking data to uniform identities throughout the enterprise. But for most countries, persuading different agencies—or even divisions within those agencies—to share a platform can be incredibly difficult.

Once again, the stumbling block is legacy infrastructure: all the hardware that's decades old, or software built before the Internet. Identity systems must be able to integrate with these ancient systems as well as future platforms as yet unbuilt.

Meanwhile, security needs vary greatly among organizations, even those headquartered in the same building. So individual agencies and departments build their own identity solutions to fit their particular needs, adding to the pileup of legacy systems. Getting these disparate platforms and applications to communicate is an enormously complex task.

The US Customs and Border Protection Agency (CBP) is a good example. At a 2015 conference, CBP chief technology officer Wolf Tombe held up the personal identity verification (PIV) card he uses to identify himself on his agency's systems and explained that, while the cards have been deployed throughout the federal government, agencies use them in vastly different and largely incompatible ways:

> Some agencies take a biometric, such as a fingerprint. Other agencies may take a retinal scan, if they're being very progressive. And some agencies don't take anything. So while the PIV cards themselves as a physical piece of infrastructure have standards, the implementation... can vary greatly between agencies.[50]

Such inconsistencies create inconvenience for citizens and a constant headache for public servants who find, for instance, that they can enter a departmental office in one city but are locked out of facilities in another. At best, hassles such as this slow people down. But if they work in a national security context, where time is often of the essence, the potential consequences could be dire.

In search of an ID solution, the US federal government has invested heavily in its Connect.gov platform, an identity management hub originally launched in 2011. Just as the Federalist platform works around siloed web design requirements, Connect.gov works around siloed identity management protocols. Individuals verify their identities with private, third-party partners, and with a single login, a citizen can access services from the Veterans Administration, US Postal Service, and numerous other agencies. Program director Jennifer Kerber says she hopes "to have government agencies organize around one sign-in platform and move away from the siloed identity-proofing they've relied on so far."[51]

Yet even if governments manage to solve the technical problems of digital identity, many of them still face an even greater challenge: convincing citizens to use them.

PRIVACY

Privacy is undoubtedly one of the biggest hurdles to modern identity management. Public opposition can be ferocious, and legislators respond to each new outcry with laws that limit or complicate agency options. Often, these laws reinforce the silos that hamper efficiency.

That said, no two countries share the same privacy context. America was founded on a healthy distrust of authority; Germans still remember the Stasi spies of the Soviet era. In these countries, opposition on privacy grounds is strong. In Asia, on the other hand, the concept of privacy is considerably different, and nations such as Singapore have had much less trouble in implementing identity management programs.

In Britain, where attitudes are similar to those in the United States, the government is trying a workaround that accommodates privacy concerns. State identity cards such as Estonia's are off the table. "This is a federated model of identity, not a centralized one," says Janet Hughes, head of policy and engagement at the Government Digital Service Identity Assurance Program. "We want to make it easier for everyone to verify their identity online, without building new, single databases or reintroducing the illiberal ID card scheme."

UK officials designed their Verify program in collaboration with privacy advocates. Rather than relying on a single authority to validate identity, British citizens can choose from a number of private-sector "identity providers." These companies use a variety of data to create strong identities, including credit reports, utility bills, driver's licenses, and mobile phone bills. As with Connect. gov, whenever you want to register for a secure government service, you simply authenticate yourself with the identity provider, which sends the government a yes/no response. The government doesn't retain your personal information or even know which provider is authenticating you, so the opportunity for abuse is limited.[52]

SECURITY

"We have been driven by our customers to provide more services online," says Don Behler, director of identity, credential, and access management at the US Social Security Administration (SSA). But "the more services we make available, the riskier those services become." Behler is describing one of the greatest challenges in digital identity: The more data the government has, the more profound the repercussions for both individuals and the government if it is misused.

The SSA is hardly alone in this regard. As the next chapter details, government agencies around the world are struggling to figure out how to secure information online—and identity is *the* critical piece of the puzzle. The problem is exacerbated by the private sector, which has made it easy to create "soft identities" that allow you to log in to and personalize websites almost effortlessly. Citizens increasingly expect the same level of convenience when interacting with government.

But the stakes for Facebook, Twitter, or Google are fairly low—none of them has to secure the person's *real* identity. Not so for government: The public sector must develop "strong identities" that allow citizens to conduct highly sensitive transactions remotely. Getting this wrong has serious real-world consequences.

Despite the difficulties, identity management is critical to any progress on digital government. Cloud computing, a cornerstone of modern government IT, provides a window on the potential for breakthroughs if identity problems are solved. Wolf Tombe, the Customs and Border Protection CTO, puts it succinctly: "Guess what the number one thing is that prevents us from going public in terms of the cloud? Security. And guess what the number one thing is in terms of security? Identity."[53]

ADOPTION

"How do you get people to buy what they don't want?" asks James Lewis, director and senior fellow at the Center for Strategic and

International Studies. "Schemes for strong authentication have come and gone over the last 20 years, from the ill-fated Clipper Chip to digital signatures, because there has been no consumer demand for them."

One problem is simply that these systems aren't mandatory. "The public has generally resisted authentication technology more complex than usernames and passwords, except when it is required," Lewis says.[54] Privacy remains a major obstacle. In many countries, people are happy to put up with analog-era government if it means keeping their data out of Big Brother's reach.

So how can governments achieve public support? By achieving *trust*. According to Gartner Research, "generating trust in the identity and access management initiatives... is vital to the success of a new digital relationship between the state and its citizens."[55] And if we look back at some of the examples in this section, that's exactly what we see. Britain's Verify system, designed with trust and privacy in mind, verified more than 140,000 identities while in its beta stage. About 100,000 people a day authenticated themselves during peak weeks of June 2015. More services are accepting Verify's endorsements.[56]

The widespread acceptance of identity management in Estonia can serve as a model. From day one, the Estonian government has gone to great lengths to engender trust in the system. It has demonstrated its commitment to accountability by giving citizens transparency and clear information about who can view their data.

CREATING VALUE

Another strategy for encouraging adoption is to create *value for citizens*. Estonia's system isn't simply a tool for single sign-on—it makes everything from visiting the hospital to boarding a train infinitely easier. If other governments want to make uniform digital identity a reality, asking their citizens to integrate an entirely new technology into their lives, they need to make it worth their while.

It's certainly worthwhile for government. "When [government] can trust more people online through the use of digital identities, it will mean more services and transactions can move online, resulting in huge cost savings," write Gary Simpson and Emma Lindley of the Open Identity Exchange.[57] People won't need to routinely call in or visit government offices. Processing times will fall as tasks start to move at the pace of computers instead of at the pace of office staff. Even corruption will decline, since you can't bribe a machine.

The challenge now is to find ways past the obstacles so that identity can be transformed from an Achilles' heel to the strong foundation that digital governments need.

CONCLUSION: MOVING SIDEWAYS

Plants and trees are anchored by taproots that grow downward, but it's their lateral roots—the ones branching out horizontally—that make them thrive by helping to collect water and nutrients. And for government systems, that's the direction to move: sideways.

Horizontally integrated government can reduce costs, improve performance, and lay the foundation for highly effective digital government. Estonia, Indiana, NIEM, and New York City show how data can foster collaboration.

Siloed departments with legacy systems remain a challenge; all that bureaucratic scar tissue will hinder growth. But as the FCC shows, agencies can both shrink it and build around it. The trick is starting small.

Like Bray, listen first. Like Flowers, consult those with field experience while exploring data. Like Hitch, create a data standard and recruit others to use it. Like the Indiana neonatal-care project, don't just expect the data to tell you answers—get on the street and *look* for them. A few key wins, early on, will help encourage trust. And without trust, the true potential for enterprise government—especially initiatives related to privacy and identity—can't be unlocked.

Of course, to really build trust, it helps if stakeholders know their data is truly secure. That's the subject of the next chapter.

CHAPTER 5 PLAYBOOK

HORIZONTAL GOVERNMENT

STRATEGIES

TACKLING DUPLICATION AND OVERLAP

Create a system of data exchanges. Creating an enterprise system is often less about trying to corral dozens of disparate agencies into using a single platform and more about creating systems of systems built around data exchanges and with a common understanding of how that shared data is defined.

Focus on people—technology is the easy part. Digital transformation in government is as much about people as it is about technology. The cultural change—fighting legacy structures and hacking down silos—will be a tough task. Get your people strategy right, and seek buy-in from key stakeholders before embarking on any large-scale transformation.

Build a common technology infrastructure. Your agency's basic IT shouldn't be a hindrance to transformation. The latest-generation devices, web and collaboration tools, and robust Wi-Fi are prerequisites to any transformation.

Phase out legacy systems gradually. You can't expect to switch on the new system and switch off the old system all at once. Instead, move users to the new system in phases, growing it with each iteration.

DATA LAYER

Use data to drive change. Data can be your biggest ally when making big changes or attempting to solve complex problems. Let the numbers do the talking; use analytics to focus your resources. Data-backed decisions are also more likely to withstand opposition and convince opponents to switch sides.

Burn down data silos. The impact of data is multiplied when data sets from across departments, domains, and sources are integrated, remixed, and processed with analytics. Make data sharing the spark that burns down silos within and between departments.

Share your success by going open-source. Building systems using open-source technologies requires a mindset shift. Start by asking: Will this system be useful to other agencies or governments with similar processes? If the answer is yes, try to develop systems based on open-source platforms and technologies.

Tap into unstructured data. Government will continue to remain the largest producer of data and, in most cases, structured data. But as you look to expand your data layer, consider tapping into unstructured sources of information such as video feeds, surveillance cameras, public tweets, and geo-tagged 311 reports.

IDENTITY MANAGEMENT

Seek public-private partnerships. Work with outside providers to verify identities. These providers pass along only the bare minimum information to government entities, often simply a yes/no response, alleviating fears of Big Brother.

Build trust by engaging with external stakeholders. Another way to defuse privacy objections is to develop identity management systems in consultation with privacy groups.

Allow citizens to opt in for better customer service. Take a cue from the US Transportation Security Agency's PreCheck program, which allows passengers who pass a background check to speed through airport security lines. In the same way, citizens who want better, faster customer service from government can opt in by giving explicit permission to share their information across agencies and levels of government.

Create stronger identities by leveraging a variety of data. While more data means more risk, it also allows citizens to create more reliable, trustworthy digital identities based on a wider range of information, thus improving overall security.

Establish a project management office for identity management. Typically each government agency manages a multitude of access management protocols. Integrating all agency-level programs under one enterprise-level PMO will not only allow you to integrate solutions and technologies across government but also expand the use of existing agency credentials.

TOOLS AND TECHNIQUES

Business architecture. Organizations operate on processes. Business architecture is an inventory of processes that can be used to help de-silo functional conversations and tie customer needs to organizational capabilities.

Proof of concept. The best way to show the advantages of hacking the silos is to start small, with a single line of business within the agency. Proving it works can help expand the horizontal movement to other areas and attract the right funding for the transformation process.

Service-enable everything. Everything IT-related should be service-enabled using application programming interfaces (APIs). These tools, which allow one computer program to communicate with another, allow a government's core IT assets to be reused and shared.

Automated refactoring. Automated refactoring provides a way to restructure and migrate multiple legacy mainframe applications into a modern environment without changing the behavior of those applications. The benefit is a low-risk, cost-effective way to migrate core business applications out of the mainframe environment.

Identity and access management gap analysis. This internal exercise maps your identity-management target state with the current state of operations, processes, and infrastructure. It highlights the gaps to address through a multiyear strategy roadmap.

RESOURCES (WEBSITES, BOOKS, AND OTHER COOL STUFF)

Open Data Now: The Secret to Hot Startups, Smart Investing, Savvy Marketing, and Fast Innovation by Joel Gurin is a good book to get you started on your open data framing.

Open Government: Collaboration, Transparency, and Participation in Practice edited by Daniel Lathrop and Laurel Ruma is a collection of more than 30 essays from government executives and thought leaders such as Matthew Burton and Tim O'Reilly. The book is available online for free at O'Reilly [http://chimera.labs.oreilly.com/books/1234000000774/index.html] and in Kindle format at GitHub. [https://github.com/oreillymedia/open_government]

The Sunlight Foundation provides a set of guidelines to address: what data should be public, how to make data public, and how to implement open data policy. There are a total of 31 recommendations peppered with examples. [http://sunlightfoundation.com/opendataguidelines/]

In addition to policy guidelines, the Sunlight Foundation is a trove of information about the open-government movement. Its blogs include *Open Data Executive Order*, *Outside the Beltway* (covering the OpenGov world beyond Washington, DC), and *Tech Tuesday* (a weekly post on use of technology to transform government). [http://sunlightfoundation.com/blog/tag/open-data-executive-order/]

CHAPTER 6

THE DARK SIDE OF HACKING:
Confronting the Cybersecurity Challenge

In the dog days of August 2015, yet another hacking scandal made the headlines. This one was huge: 33 million customer records stolen from AshleyMadison.com, a site designed to facilitate extramarital affairs. Nearly 10 gigabytes of member data were held hostage for nearly a month by hackers who claimed to have stolen the database and then dumped it onto the Dark Web and various peer-to-peer file-sharing sites. Names, addresses, phone numbers, credit card numbers, transactions, and links to member profiles—*everything* was revealed.

The Ashley Madison hack wasn't just big, it was different. When a government's or company's servers are breached, most of the ensuing costs are related to identity theft, negative brand impacts, or financial or intellectual property loss. But for Ashley Madison customers, the cost was much more personal. As the hackers put it, "Chances are your man signed up on the world's biggest affair site, but never had one. He just tried to. If that distinction matters."[1]

For 33 million people, that distinction does matter—a lot. "The Ashley Madison hack is in some ways the first large-scale real hack, in the popular, your-secrets-are-now-public sense of the word," writes John Herrman of the Awl. "It is plausible—likely?— that you will know someone in or affected by this dump," he says.[2]

It wouldn't be such a big deal if the data were merely leaked onto the black market; the possibility of it coming back to haunt any one individual would be fairly low. But within hours of the release, coders had already built websites where anyone could type in an email address and see if it was in the database.

This raises a number of vexing questions, Herrman says:

> If the names and email addresses are available in a simple Google-like search, for example, will they search for their partners? Friends? Co-workers? Representatives? Family members? If so, why? If not, why not? Will you seek out the raw leak data after reading this post? Will news organizations, present-ed with user profiles associated with public figures, ask for comment? Treat each as news? Which ones? How?[3]

For many, the answers to these questions proved painful, even life-changing. Several suicides followed the revelations.[4] For Ashley Madison, the hack began what are likely to be years of litigation at mind-boggling expense.

How did the company find itself in this mess? And more importantly—other than the 15,000 .gov and .mil addresses found in the Ashley Madison database—why is this relevant to government?

Surprisingly, Ashley Madison and governments have much in common concerning cybersecurity, even if they're worlds apart in mission. Perhaps the greatest similarity is that both store highly sensitive data that could be lucrative in the hands of criminals.

The challenges to government, however, run deeper. Government stores far more data than the private sector, and, as seen in the previous chapter, often keeps it on older, more vulnerable systems. Governments are targeted not just by opportunistic hackers but also by determined teams funded and trained by nation-states. And even as governments try to protect themselves against hostile intruders, employees and citizens alike want their data conveniently available anytime, anywhere.

Without better cybersecurity and trust in government's ability to secure data, digital transformation will fall short. Cybersecurity, then, is perhaps the greatest challenge to the vision described in this book. Let's consider how it can be addressed.

GOVERNMENT: THE BIGGEST TARGET

"In the early days of criminal hacking, it was about showing what was possible—breaking into systems for fun and the challenge," explains security expert Marc Goodman, the author of the book *Future Crimes*, one of the most detailed accounts of the massive cybercrime marketplace. "[But] later, a profit motive emerged, which attracted criminal elements that were serious, organized, and global. As a result, the US now classifies cyberspace as a new domain of battle—as significant as air, land, or sea."[5]

It's not hard to see why. For every Ashley Madison, we see just as many headlines about governments being breached. Frankly, it's surprising there aren't more. In 2013, the energy company BP said it experienced about 50,000 attempts at cyberintrusion per day. The Pentagon reports more than 10 million daily attempts, as does the National Nuclear Security Administration. States are big targets too.[6] All in all, the public sector faces more security incidents and data breaches than any other sector.[7]

In short, government cybersecurity presents a unique problem simply due to the huge volume of cybersecurity threats government agencies face on a daily basis. And the threats are also unique in their potential for enormous costs and disastrous consequences.

One of the highest-profile recent examples was a 2014 breach at the US Office of Personnel Management (OPM). Personnel records and security-clearance files for at least 22 million people were compromised.[8] The data were extremely sensitive: Security applications are 127 pages long and contain everything from mental health history to criminal records, financial data, drug and alcohol use, assignment/work history, family member names, personal references, and fingerprints. With this kind of detail, officials have said it's likely that foreign governments will try to use the data to identify US operatives, particularly those in intelligence roles.[9]

Experts rank this breach as one of the most damaging in US history—so far. "It is a very big deal from a national security perspective and from a counterintelligence perspective," says FBI director James B. Comey. "It's a treasure trove of information about everybody who has worked for, tried to work for, or works for the United States government."[10] Security veteran John Watters calls it "a huge national loss [that] will have ramifications for years to come."[11]

The OPM hack, and most cyberthreats, look a lot like bank robberies. Attackers make a narrow, targeted intrusion to steal lots of data. Yet all-out assaults could be even worse than targeted strikes and more immediately catastrophic. In the words of the *Washington Post*, "Sophisticated and virtually untraceable political 'hacktivists' may now possess the ability to disrupt or destroy government operations, banking transactions, city power grids, and even military weapon systems."[12]

Put both types of attacks together, and you have a recipe for nationwide chaos.

Believe it or not, though, disruption on this scale has already happened. In 2007, Estonia found itself the target of a weeks-long, all-out cyberattack by Russian hackers angry at the removal of the Bronze Soldier of Tallinn, a famous Soviet statue, from the capital. What began with sharp rhetoric and mild protests became a serious economic offensive when Russian Internet forums urged sympathetic hackers to act. Soon, the computer networks of Estonian banks, government agencies, and media outlets began failing. ATMs were knocked offline. It became so serious that the country actually had to "pull the plug," severing access to all Estonian websites from abroad.

"The episode has since been dubbed the world's first cyberwar, or Cyber War I," Kertu Ruus wrote the following year in the journal *European Affairs*, "because it was the first time that a sustained, wholesale, and politically motivated e-assault was launched to wreak havoc on a country's entire digital infrastructure."[13]

Of course, this was an extreme case. Most government hacks are subtler, stealing Social Security numbers or tax returns, not crashing entire economies. You may not hear about them in the news, but such intrusions happen all the time, and not just at the Department of Defense. States and cities are being targeted as well.

In South Carolina, for instance, sometime in late summer 2012, Eastern European hackers hit servers at the state's Department of Revenue, sucking up Social Security and credit card numbers in bulk. A state worker had fallen for a phishing email, which looks legitimate but harbors computer-breaching malware. The worker clicked on a link in the email that allowed the hackers to steal login and password information, opening the door to the revenue department's servers. By the time the state discovered and closed the breach on October 10, the hackers had vacuumed up 3.6 million Social Security numbers and 400,000 credit card numbers.[14]

In this case, the hackers' motive was clearly financial. Social Security and credit card numbers can be sold on a network of illegal trading sites. The majority of today's cyberattacks fit this description. A recent report by the RAND Corporation found that in many ways, the market built around this type of heist has become more profitable than the illegal drug trade.[15] With the rise of cyberspace as a battlefield, however, attacks with political aims are increasingly common.

Whatever the motive, it's clear that governments are the highest-value targets for hackers today. Thus, it's critical that they invest in strong cyberdefenses—stronger, if anything, than those found in the private sector. At the state and local levels in particular, however, most agencies simply aren't devoting enough manpower and funding to the problem.

More than three-fourths of state chief information security officers in the United States say their states aren't spending enough on cybersecurity, and attracting and retaining the right talent continues to be difficult due to the usual problems: lower salaries, a lack of clear career paths, and convoluted hiring processes.[16] But it's also an issue of strategy, which means knowing your adversary.

TOOLS OF THE TRADE

Hacking wasn't always a criminal enterprise. In the early days, it was all about having fun and impressing your peers. Apple co-founders Steve Wozniak and Steve Jobs were early hackers, "phone phreakers" who learned to manipulate telephone systems and trick the phone company into giving out free long-distance calls. For Jobs, hacking was very much about the sense of adventure: "It was the magic of the fact that two teenagers could build this box for $100 worth of parts and control hundreds of billions of dollars of infrastructure in the entire telephone network of the whole world."[17]

Today, however, ego triumphs have largely been replaced by the lure of profit in the form of stolen data—and the cash you can make with it.

Unsurprisingly, the opportunity attracts organized crime. Marc Goodman writes, "Organized crime groups around the world have created a vast and highly efficient underground economy in which the stolen data is exploited by networks of geographically disparate crime syndicates."[18] And the losses have been catastrophic: security firm McAfee estimates the global cost to companies and consumers at between $375 billion and $500 billion annually.[19]

At the heart of this underground economy are black markets, bazaars where any kind of digital thievery can be commissioned. When a syndicate wants a hack, it can outsource for capabilities it lacks, or simply contract for the whole job. In fact, many "hackers" today don't do any real hacking. They buy and coordinate the services of others, and then sit back to watch the damage unfold.

These markets live on the so-called Dark Web—the Internet's Wild West, which can't be accessed with traditional browsers or search engines. RAND's National Security Research Division recently studied these markets and found exponential growth in the past 10 to 15 years:

> Almost any computer-literate person can enter the market. With the increase of as-a-service models and do-it-yourself kits (with easy-to-use administration

panels), anyone can deploy variants of malware. One can buy credentials, credit cards, and personally identifiable information (PII) without needing to be highly technical.

These technologies have massively lowered the barriers to entry, leading to marketplaces with up to 80,000 members and global revenues in the hundreds of millions of dollars.[20]

Incredibly, notes Goodman, hackers can even learn how to launch phishing and spamming campaigns through massive open online courses (MOOCs) specifically tailored to the criminal class. "Hackers are not born," he says. "They are trained, supported, and self-taught by an enormous amount of free educational material in the digital underground."[21]

The boom in hacking has led to skyrocketing sales for hacking tools, like the sales of picks and shovels during a gold rush. And, as in the gold rush, there may be as much money to be made in creating hacking tools as in the actual thefts.

In 2006, RAND found only one new "exploit kit"—a toolbox for finding security flaws and introducing malware—entering the market. By 2013, 33 new tools for distributing and managing attacks had emerged. This means organizations face not only an increasing number of attacks but also an increasing variety of them. Goodman says many of the organizations offering these tools have become so sophisticated that they actually use customer relationship management to track customer requests and build brand loyalty among their criminal clients.[22]

The goods and services available on these markets span many categories, covering every stage in the life cycle of a hack:

CATEGORY	DESCRIPTION	EXAMPLES
Initial access tools	Allow users to perform arbitrary operations on a machine and deliver payloads	• Exploits • Zero-day vulnerabilities
Payload parts and features	Goods or services that create, package, or enhance payloads to gain a foothold into a system	• Packers • Crypters • Binders
Payloads	Impart malicious behavior, including data destruction, service denial, deception, or data exfiltration	• Botnets for sale
Enabling services	Assist users in finding targets or driving them to a desired destination for an initial access tool or payload	• Spam services • Phishing and spear-phishing services • Fake websites
Full services	Packages of all the above items; the full attack life cycle	• Hackers for hire • Botnets for rent • Doxing • DDoS as a service
Enabling and operations support products	Ensure that initial access tools and hacking services will work as needed and can overcome obstacles	• Infrastructure • Cryptanalytic services • CAPTCHA breaking
Digital assets	Items obtained from the target or victim (stolen information)	• Credit card information • Account information • PII/PH
Digital asset commerce and cyberlaundering	Facilitate the sale of digital assets	• Mule services • Counterfeit goods and services • Card cloners • Forwarding products services

Source: RAND Corporation[23]

And these tools are just the beginning. The future looks bright for hackers, Goodman says:

> Imminent fundamental shifts in computing, including the emergence of ubiquitous computing and the "Internet of Things," will yet again exponentially drive growth in big data. As companies gather more and more data from more and more devices… criminals will have an ever-expanding pool of targets from which to choose.[24]

This raises key questions about how governments should handle cybersecurity. It's increasingly clear that perfect cybersecurity is impossible. Every gigabyte you store is a gigabyte at risk. Knowing this, is preserving more and more data really a good idea? Or do the potential costs outweigh the benefits?

ADDRESSING THE CYBERSECURITY CHALLENGE

Cybersecurity threats are growing in volume, intensity, and sophistication, and they aren't going away—ever. Yet government *could* protect itself much better than it does today.

Recent failures, in fact, call into question the effectiveness of the billions already sunk into cybersecurity. How can government agencies reverse the growing gap between security investment and effectiveness? Traditionally, cybersecurity has focused on preventing intrusions, defending firewalls, monitoring ports, and the like. The evolving threat landscape, however, calls for a more dynamic approach.

New thinking in this arena involves three fundamental capabilities:

- **Security**: Prioritize risks and enhance controls to protect against known and emerging threats.
- **Vigilance**: Detect violations and anomalies through better monitoring of workplace behaviors.
- **Resilience**: Establish the ability to quickly return to normal operations and repair damage to business.[25]

These three principles reflect the fact that cyberdefense mechanisms must evolve. Government agencies can't rely on perimeter security alone, and they should also build strong capabilities for detection, response, reconnaissance, and recovery. The SANS Institute, which performs security training and research, codifies this as a guiding principle: "Prevention is ideal, but detection is a must."[26] With strong detection, agencies can catch incidents early and prepare for their aftermath. And given Estonia's experience after removing the Soviet statue, you can see why effective recovery plans are important.

Furthermore, officials must be wary of the celebrated mindset that failure isn't an option. Instead, they should accept risk while trying to minimize it as much as possible, especially for top-priority information. As Ed Powers writes in the *WSJ Risk & Compliance Journal*:

> The reality is that cyber risk is not something that can be avoided; instead, it must be managed. By understanding what data is most important, management can then determine what investments in security controls might be needed to protect those critical assets.[27]

SECURITY

Government agencies need to examine and understand all aspects of their operations in cyberspace. The first step is simple: They need to *lock the doors*. Too many government agencies are leaving these doors ajar without even realizing it.

But you can't be sure all your doors are closed if you don't know where they are. This is a problem many governments have with IT systems. "Most agencies don't even know what IT systems they have," says Alan Paller, founder of the SANS Institute.[28] Similarly, agencies must review their data to determine levels of sensitivity. Public data such as school bus schedules should be stored differently than medical histories. Biometric records are even more sensitive and deserve a higher tier of protection.

Closing doors also means taking simple steps such as two-factor authentication (typically, a card and a password or ID number) and encryption for sensitive data. For extremely sensitive information such as the OPM data, says John Watters, "you have that data decentralized, much of it offline with very tight controls and accesses." Forget convenience and focus on security, he says: "You take those databases offline. Make them hard to access. You place air gaps between them."[29]

Part of the problem is a lack of accountability. It's hard to decide who takes the blame in a government security breach. Among CIOs, executives, and security departments, responsibility becomes diffuse. "The key is accountability, and the key to making accountability work is measurement tools," Paller says. Departments need "cyberhygiene" policies designed to protect systems from hackers and malware such as automatic upgrades and patching. Automated programs then can measure compliance and keep leaders informed.

Another problem is that managers often don't understand how cybersecurity works. A bank's CEO may know how trades and transactions work all the way down to the teller. But he or she generally won't have that kind of knowledge about the IT department.

Outside the technology sector, most leaders and managers have *no* background in software code and little detailed understanding of cyber issues. The problem is even more acute in the general workforce. Even when a government IT staff does an admirable job in closing all the doors, employees may keep opening them back up inadvertently—or intentionally. This is the *insider threat*, and for many organizations, it's one of the biggest threats they face.

When most people consider this risk, they may think of Edward Snowden, leaking classified information from the US National Security Agency (NSA)—what's called a malicious insider threat. Yet while disgruntled employees are a serious threat to government, so too are those who break security through ignorance or complacency. The systems administrator who plays Minecraft in a secure environment and clicks on a link for the latest update—which is actually malware—has just let the bad guys into the agency's systems. The consequence is equally devastating, whether intentional or not.

Fortunately, the advent of big data and sophisticated analytics gives governments ways to counteract the insider threat. Today's tools can detect anomalous actions by employees that deviate from peer-group practices or their own previous behavior. Such behavioral analytics allow organizations to flag suspicious emails and badge check-ins, downloads, and access to unauthorized sites and assets.

Consider this example: An employee receives several negative performance evaluations, takes to social media to express his dissatisfaction, and downloads data from internal systems without approval. He moves large amounts of these sensitive data into the cloud after normal business hours. Then he schedules personal time off in a foreign country he hasn't visited before. Organizations with new analytical tools can identify and investigate such anomalies and, in the best case, intercept the employee before he leaves.

Whether it's an inside or external threat, organizations are finding that building firewalls is less effective than anticipating the nature of threats—which means studying malware in the wild, before it exploits a vulnerability. This can be achieved by harnessing the power of collective intelligence.

Simply put, the evolving nature of cyberthreats calls for a collaborative, networked defense. This means sharing information about vulnerabilities, threats, and remedies among a community of governments, companies, and security vendors. Promoting this kind of exchange between the public and private sectors was a key aim of the US Cyber Security Act of 2012.[30]

Australia has taken a significant lead in working across government and the private sector to shore up collective defenses. The Australian Cyber Security Centre (ACSC) tries to ensure that Australian networks are among the world's most secure. It plays many roles, raising awareness of cybersecurity, reporting on the nature and extent of cyberthreats, encouraging reporting of cybersecurity incidents, analyzing and investigating specific threats, coordinating national cybersecurity operations, and heading up the Australian government's response to hacking incidents. At its core, it's a hub for information exchange. Private companies, state and territorial governments, and international partners all share discoveries at ACSC.[31]

The Australian approach begins with good network hygiene. The government encourages organizations to follow three best practices:

- **Application whitelisting**—Protect against unauthorized and malicious programs by blocking all unknown executable files and software libraries.
- **Prompt patching**—Automatically run software updates for all programs on all computers, including operating systems, to ensure that security patches occur as quickly as possible.
- **Limited administrative privileges**—Those with administrative privileges often can make virtually any change and retrieve almost any information, making them high-value targets. Restricting such privileges and tightly controlling their use can counter this threat.[32]

These are the basics of what's needed to keep the doors locked against cybercriminals. They're mandatory practice for all Australian government entities.

After the doors are locked, it's worthwhile to assess your adversaries. Australia's program combines threat data from multiple entities to strengthen collective intelligence. The results of intrusion attempts are uploaded to the cloud, giving analysts from multiple agencies a larger pool of attack data to scan for patterns.

Collective intelligence revealed its value during the 2001 fight against the Lion worm, which exploited a vulnerability in computer connections.[33] A few analysts noticed a spike in probes to port 53, which supports the Domain Name Service, the system for naming computers and network servers organized around domains. They warned international colleagues, who collaborated on a response. Soon, a system administrator in the Netherlands collected a sample of the worm, which allowed other experts to examine it in a protected testing environment, a "sandbox." A global community of security practitioners then identified the worm's mechanism and built a program to detect infections. In 14 hours, they publicized their findings widely enough to defend computers worldwide.

A third core security principle is to rethink network security. All too often, leaders think of it as a wall. But a Great Wall can be scaled; a Maginot Line can be avoided. Fixed obstacles are fixed targets. That's not optimal cyberdefense. Instead, think of cybersecurity like a chess match. Governments need to deploy their advantages and strengths against their opponents' disadvantages and weaknesses.

Perpetual unpredictability is the best defense. Keep moving. Keep changing. No sitting; no stopping. Plant fake information. Deploy "honeypots" (decoy servers or systems). Move data around. If criminals get in, flood them with bad information. The goal is to modify the defenses so fast that hackers waste money and time probing systems that have already changed. Savvy cybersecurity pros understand this; the more you change the game, the more your opponents' costs go up, and the more your costs go down. Maybe they'll move on to an easier target.

"Most people want to build [a defense] and let it sit for two years," says cybersecurity consultant Craig Astrich, but that doesn't work. "This is a constant evolution," he says. Agencies need to learn to love continuous change. As Astrich says, "I'm putting myself out of my job as fast as I can every day."[34] New problems will arise. There'll always be work.

UNDERSTANDING THE THREAT

The language of digital crime and espionage is certainly colorful—"phishing," "pharming," "war dialing," "smurf attacks," and "the ping of death"; "zombie systems," "botnets," "rootkits," and "Trojans." But if the language is playful, the consequences of cyberattack can be devastating.

The public sector's difficulties in defending against these attacks are well known. But a new generation of warriors is going on the offense by investigating the tactics and targets of cybercriminals. Known as "cyber reconnaissance" (CR) and "threat intelligence," this emerging antihacker discipline is infiltrating the Dark Web in an aggressive effort to anticipate, neutralize, and disrupt hackers— or at least offer their targets a warning.

"The fundamental problem is, how do you find signals in the noise, and figure out which one of those alerts created the biggest risk for your enterprise?" John Watters says.[35] The answer, say Watters and other cyber experts, is deep intelligence on hacker networks, from malware vendors to stolen credit card buyers. By understanding their methods, the thinking goes, governments can better anticipate and recognize future risks, stopping hacks before they start.

The CR offensive is promising, yet dramatic ambushes of would-be hackers remain rare. For now, the conflict between cyber recon and the Dark Web is more like trench warfare: CR experts try to figure out what cybercriminals are doing, while the criminals hustle to find new ways to circumvent changing systems.

With investment, experience, and a growing army of CR operatives, the stalemate may change. One way to tip the scales in their favor is to aggressively adopt another key component of cyber reconnaissance: examining security defenses from the outside in, seeing them the way the bad guys do.

This goes well beyond simply probing systems for vulnerabilities. It means understanding which data are the most desirable to the bad guys, which cybercriminals would be most interested in their data, and which hacks they're most likely to use to infiltrate systems.

As with modern-day terrorism, cybersecurity has proven daunting because the nature of the threat is constantly evolving. It requires staying ahead of the trajectories of multiple technologies and the threats associated with each. Each major technological development—mobile, social, cloud computing—brings a host of new risks. And typically, in the early stages of these technologies, innovators focus less on security than on creating a minimum viable product.

Cybercriminals, on the other hand, are laser-focused on exploiting new technologies before developers discover their vulnerabilities. Governments should make significant efforts to study emerging threats, looking at key risk indicators and understanding the actors—criminals, foreign countries, and hacktivists—who threaten government systems.

The Internet of Things (IoT) presents limitless possibilities for businesses and governments alike. The US General Services Administration (GSA), for example, has equipped several of its buildings with a sensor network aimed at reducing energy use and wasted resources. The sensors raise shades or dim bulbs based on how much sunlight enters a room. They detect motion and turn off extra lights and air-conditioning when employees leave their desks. They collect data on daily energy and water consumption.[36] Cities around the world are experimenting with "smart" parking, street lighting, and environmental monitoring, among other applications—all of them relying on sensors, data, and connected devices.

Unfortunately, the IoT's chief strength is also its chief vulnerability. A connected device lends itself to hacking. A connected lamp could provide a point of access to an entire private network—and imagine the value to an assassin of knowing whether a diplomat is at her desk. Hackers might bring down complete systems in minutes. Gartner, the IT research company, expects the number of connected devices to reach 25 billion by 2020, compounding the number of vulnerable targets to an unprecedented scale.

The IoT also introduces new types of risk. For example, the manufacturing of fraudulent imitations of sensors lacking security controls. IoT-enabled processes, furthermore, may operate across multiple organizations and third-party systems, and inadequate security at one vendor could pose a risk to the entire network.

Understanding these risks is a first step toward safeguarding the IoT. But there are other steps all organizations should take to secure their devices:

- **Define uniform standards for interoperability.** Develop a single set of standards for *all* members of a network, and stick to it. This will help ensure that devices work together safely and effectively.
- **Use purpose-built devices rather than pre-IoT solutions.** Organizations should strongly consider new, secure technologies designed specifically for the

IoT. It's a safer option than retrofitting or expanding old systems designed under different conditions for different purposes.

- **Designate responsibilities for participants in your ecosystem.** Rather than sharing responsibility across an ecosystem, make individuals and organizations aware of exactly what they're personally responsible for protecting.
- **Establish baseline data.** View IoT systems broadly, monitoring environmental characteristics such as usage, location, and access. This can establish a baseline for distinguishing between normal and suspicious activity.
- **Provide data governance.** Guidance on how data should be collected, used, and stored can prevent unwanted breaches—and prevent a risk event from escalating into something larger.[37]

It may turn out that managing risk for the IoT calls for an entirely new approach—and FCC CIO David Bray thinks he has one. Drawing from his experience preparing for bioterrorism at the US Centers for Disease Control and Prevention (CDC), Bray says public health can provide a model for cybersecurity.

"Consider approaching cybersecurity differently—focusing instead on cyber resiliency and an approach more akin to 'cyber public health' aimed at both preventive measures and rapid detection, containment, and mitigation of cyberthreats akin to infectious disease control," Bray writes in a blog post. Just as anonymized and aggregated health data help public health agencies understand and fight disease outbreaks, Bray believes a "cyber CDC" could "protect privacy and improve resiliency by anonymously sharing the equivalent of cyber signs, symptoms, and behaviors that different [IoT] devices are experiencing."[38]

Next, let's explore just what such an approach might look like and how to institutionalize it.

RESILIENCE: BOUNCING BACK

Doctors say prevention is better than cure. They're right, but prevention sometimes fails. What if, despite vaccines, you get the flu? That's when your body's resilience kicks in, fighting the infection and restoring your health. Bodies generally have a zero-tolerance policy toward pathogens, accelerating blood flow and increasing body temperature to create an inhospitable environment for them. The identity, source, and intent of the threat is irrelevant; the focus is on isolating and attacking it.

Similarly, an organization's resilience to cyberattack can be what saves it when disaster strikes. The need to detect intrusion and quarantine it becomes paramount. Cyberforensics can study and trace the threat in a controlled environment, away from business systems. This sort of detective work requires a vastly different mindset than the perimeter-defense approach.

How and how quickly organizations react to cyberattack can determine the extent to which they can minimize further damage, neutralize threats, and recover. Resilience means the capacity to rapidly contain damage and mobilize diverse resources to minimize its impact.

Organizations shouldn't have to suffer a real crisis to find out they're inadequately equipped to cope with one. That's why cyber war-gaming is so useful. Cyber war-gaming immerses participants in simulated cyberattack scenarios, such as a data breach, website defacement, denial-of-service attack, or sophisticated malware on a network. Although infinitely more sophisticated and complex, a war game serves the same purpose as a fire drill, gauging the organization's speed and readiness and giving employees a chance to practice their responses. It also helps earn executive buy-in for cyber risk programs by elevating their importance in the minds of department leaders.

So how does a cyber war game work? It begins with an elaborate scenario. A group of executives is assigned to play the role of a response team for a fictional organization, such as a global pharmaceutical giant or a public agency. The executives are presented with a mock attack on their systems and asked to develop a response and recovery plan. To do this, they'll have to answer a variety of questions: How did the intruders get in? What's the extent of damage? How can the breach be contained? How can damage to reputation be minimized?

To complicate matters further, the responders must cope with a continuing flow of new information that may not always be accurate. They need to manage and communicate with stakeholders—clients, a board of directors, business partners, the media, and staff—while racing against the clock.[39] As the war game unfolds, critical insights and lessons come to light.

For example, instead of putting the agency head in charge by default, designate a crisis officer to run the attack response. This can help ensure that it's executed according to plan and minimize the chance that day-to-day politics will interfere. Another key challenge is information. When a cyberthreat hits, information—

especially reliable information—is scarce. It's important for response teams to realize this and avoid decisions based entirely on first impressions. In all, the war game exercise can help all parties involved appreciate the importance of discipline and agility.[40]

Resilience isn't built overnight. It takes practice. War-gaming is a safe way to establish the "muscle memory" and coordination needed to manage a potential crisis.[41]

A resilient organization minimizes access rights so that, in the event of a breach, only a small amount of information can be leaked. It encrypts and anonymizes data to restrict its availability and usefulness. It continually scans for breaches so that it can identify leaks as soon as possible.

Resilience is also about rebuilding trust. Utah's governor Gary Herbert immediately accepted the responsibility when his state's IT department exposed about 750,000 people's medical records, including some Social Security information. His immediate mea culpa overstated the damage but restored citizen confidence.

But rebuilding trust also requires concrete steps. South Carolina's Department of Revenue hack ultimately led to better security. A few high-profile firings and new standards helped to spark a cultural shift; today, a new division of information security helps manage security across all government departments. The state's computers have dual-protected logins, meaning they require another form of authentication beyond the user's password. In addition, South Carolina has implemented broad cybersecurity monitoring to detect potential incursions that penetrate the initial defense layers.

CLOSING THE CYBERSKILLS GAP

A cybersecurity strategy means nothing without the skills and talent needed to execute it. Technology companies and banks with world-class cybersecurity capabilities owe much of their success to top-flight technical staff. While the defense and intelligence sectors generally can attract high-caliber talent, other federal, state, and local agencies find it difficult to compete with the private sector. In fact, a talent shortage is consistently cited as one of the key challenges to better public cybersecurity.[42]

For government agencies that think millennials will save the day, think again. A 2014 Raytheon survey found that few Americans between ages 18 and 26 are inclined toward cybersecurity work. Nearly two-thirds of respondents said that no guidance counselor or teacher had ever mentioned it as a potential career.[43]

Governments must cast a wider net to address the need for cybersecurity professionals. One interesting approach is the University of South Florida's Florida Center for Cybersecurity. Its 36-week program is designed to train students for lucrative jobs in cybersecurity. With classes slated to begin in spring 2016, the first graduates can't come soon enough; experts say employers offering more than 200,000 cybersecurity jobs nationwide are competing for 4,000 to 5,000 qualified candidates.[44] And as more and more high-profile cyberattacks make the front page, the need will only continue to increase.

The US Cyber Challenge (USCC) offers another promising model for boosting the supply of cybersecurity professionals. Led by Karen Evans, former federal CIO, the organization's mission is to recruit and place the next generation of cybersecurity professionals.

USCC's competitions are designed to identify the nation's most promising candidates for a variety of information security disciplines. Its 2015 competition, for example, emphasized secure coding. "By developing and implementing our competitions and programs, USCC is drawing talent out of the shadows and giving them platforms to build upon their skill sets, connect with others in the field, and find careers that put their capabilities to work while defending our nation," Evans says.[45]

The winners of USCC's online cybersecurity competitions spend a week at a cybercamp offering intensive training in cyber-security from leading experts. These camps serve individuals college-aged and older from any profession. "We have all kinds of different people coming through the camps," says Evans. Campers have ranged in age from 16 to 65. The only limits on participation are minimum age, US citizenship, and a high score in the online qualifying competition.

South Korea uses a similar model. To defend against constant cyberattacks from North Korea, the state trains teams of teenagers in cybersecurity and pits them against one another in mock war games. The tournaments are similar to Korea's popular video game competitions; each team has to respond to an incursion modeled after a real North Korean hack.[46] The tournament lures talent with substantial prize money and job preferences. Winners also may be tracked into technology fields when they begin South Korea's compulsory military service.

Experts agree that cybersecurity requires different skill sets than other IT work. While coding skills are valuable, network security requires a talent for understanding systems and getting into the heads of adversaries. The talent search has been likened to trying to find the rare child who, instead of playing with toys, prefers to dismantle them.

It's a different headspace than an engineer's instinct to fix problems. You have to anticipate vulnerabilities. "You have a working system, and you need to figure out how it's going to be perturbed and broken," says Paller. That's one reason why the Defense Intelligence Agency is recruiting liberal arts students who show aptitude at sleuthing out the motives and means of malicious hackers.[47]

With an eye to the future, the US government is indexing all of its IT jobs, from network administration to web design.[48] The hope is that a systematic chart of job responsibilities and requirements will make it easier for young talent to explore specific tech career tracks, including those that defend the nation's data.

CONCLUSION: MANAGING CYBER RISK

The Internet is a new environment with its own rules and its own dangers. In the past two decades, we've connected our economy and society via the Internet—a platform designed primarily for *sharing* information, not protecting it. This connectivity has driven innovation and high performance in the public and private sectors alike.

Yet even as connectivity reshapes government in positive ways, it also presents growing business opportunities for criminals with cybertalents. As governments extend their capabilities through cloud computing, IT outsourcing and partnerships, they increase their reliance on complex infrastructure not fully within their control. Similarly, government efforts to engage citizens and employees through social media introduce new gaps and opportunities attackers will try to exploit.

Like legitimate governments, cybercriminals, hacktivists, and nation-states are also using the Internet to expand their reach. With every step governments take toward protecting their online operations, hackers will be close behind.

In short, digital strategies inevitably introduce new risks. Yet when one considers the inherent link between performance, innovation, and risk, it becomes clear that overly tight controls could impede important strategic initiatives.

The only way forward, then, is to accept that some break-ins will occur. Living with risk is the new normal, and managing it is an *essential* part of achieving optimal performance in digital government.

This challenge for governments resembles that facing military strategists as their primary roles shift from war against established nations to continual skirmishes against elusive, unpredictable non-state actors. Your government will inevitably lose some cybersecurity skirmishes, but that doesn't mean it's failed. It's a given that not every encounter will end in victory.

The important test lies in how government officials anticipate and counter moves by an ever-shifting cast of criminal adversaries. Digital governments will need speed, dexterity, and adaptability to succeed on this new battlefield.

CHAPTER 6 PLAYBOOK

CONFRONTING THE CYBERSECURITY CHALLENGE

SUCCESS STRATEGIES

SECURE STRATEGIES

Identify the most attractive data targets for attackers. Gather your business leaders and threat intelligence experts and have them identify the top areas of cyber risk for your agency. Use this information to create policies that protect the most valuable data with the highest level and number of privacy and security controls.

Use enterprise-level privacy officers to identify weak spots. Privacy officers can help determine which citizen data needs to be protected and why. They also play an important role in safeguarding citizen privacy and restoring trust when an incident occurs.

Monitor and audit third-party providers. Working with IT vendors is almost inevitable, but don't assume vendors are complying with the data privacy and security stipulations in work agreements. *Confirm* their compliance, and identify and address weaknesses in their systems and processes.

VIGILANT STRATEGIES

Stay up to date on the full range of tactics attackers employ. Expect attackers to be creative. Expect breaches to occur, and create multiple layers of protection to render some breaches harmless. Remember that attackers and their tools are becoming increasingly sophisticated. Staying aware of their strategies is an important first step toward gaining advantage over them.

Identify potential external and internal threats and risk profiles. Step into the shoes of potential security threats to better grasp the precautions you need to thwart them. Analyze their capabilities, interests, and motivations. In the event of a cyberattack, these exercises will help you respond more effectively to reduce its impact.

Improve risk management through collective intelligence. Share information about vulnerabilities, threats, and remedies to build a cybercommunity of governments, enterprises and security vendors. Such collective intelligence can direct security audits and cyber-forensics to areas of known or suspected weakness. And it can reveal trends and suggest areas where additional security measures are warranted.

RESILIENT STRATEGIES

Create cyberaware employee user experiences. The best of these have security attributes so tightly integrated as to be barely notice-able. Organizations that pay attention to user experience as they design their employee educational programs can quietly and unobtrusively guide users toward more vigilant and resilient behaviors.

Run simulations to glean insights on readiness. A resilient cyber risk management system isn't built in a day. It requires constant tweaking and iterations to make it battle ready. You need to run regular "fire drill" simulations on your system to understand its weaknesses and improve it continually.

Evolve defense mechanisms. You can't rely on protection of the perimeter alone. Develop threat-monitoring plans for early detection of incidents and be prepared to respond when incidents do occur. Have an effective recovery plan so that operations can be up and running quickly after a cyberincident.

Identify your cyberattack point person. Choose a crisis officer to run the response during an all-out cyberattack.

STAKEHOLDER AND TALENT STRATEGIES

Communicate the growing complexity of cyberthreats. Clearly convey the nature and severity of cyber risks to agency and legislative leaders and other stakeholders. Simply reporting on the progress and success of cyberinitiatives isn't enough.

Use private-sector partnerships to plug cyberskills gaps. Identify the skills and competencies you need to make your agency cyberready. Provide training that allows your employees to effectively manage teams including members from outside government. Third-party partnerships may cover activities ranging from managing security functions to providing specialists as needed.

Make cybersecurity an attractive career option in government. Begin by mapping cybersecurity competencies and creating well-documented job descriptions. Work with a dedicated cyber HR professional to redefine the cybersecurity career path and create strong learning programs that develop and grow the right talent from the start.

TOOLS AND TECHNIQUES

Cyber war-gaming. Create interactive cyberattack scenarios and immerse potential responders in them to evaluate preparedness and identify deficiencies. Cyber war-gaming can help government agencies develop a shared perception of security threats and response needs.

Attack graph. Understand vulnerabilities within the network by depicting the ways in which an adversary can break in. Attack graphs can help system administrators analyze weaknesses in the system and develop and deploy measures to improve them.

Whitelisting. This requires the software to determine whether software is included in a "trusted" list and whether it will be allowed to run. It allows only trusted content and software to run on your system.

Honeypots and honey nets. These are fake computer systems used to dupe attackers and collect information on intruders. They can be good learning tools if used correctly, but require substantial resources.

Penetration test. This is an intentional attack on a computer system to understand its weaknesses and find ways to gain access to its features and data. The goal is to learn about loopholes in the system and develop strategies to mitigate them.

RESOURCES (WEBSITES, BOOKS, AND OTHER COOL STUFF)

Future Crimes: Everything Is Connected, Everyone Is Vulnerable, and What We Can Do About It by Marc Goodman illuminates the critical nature of cyberthreats.

Enterprise Security: A Data-Centric Approach to Securing the Enterprise by Aaron Woody explains how to use data to enhance security.

The US Computer Emergency Readiness Team (US-CERT) has an informational page on common security issues for non-technical computer users. You can also sign up to receive tips in your inbox. [https://www.us-cert.gov/ncas/tips]

The US Department of Homeland Security's National Initiative for Cybersecurity Careers and Studies (NICCS) has developed a standard approach for cybersecurity work and workforces. [https://niccs.us-cert.gov/training/national-cybersecurity-workforce-framework] NICCS also maintains a repository of more than 1,300 cybersecurity-related courses and training programs. [https://niccs.us-cert.gov/training/tc/search]

The SANS Institute is a cooperative research and education organization for cybersecurity professionals that offers classroom and online training programs. [https://www.sans.org/online-security-training/]

You can also access a plethora of newsletters, websites, and other resources focused primarily on security issues.

- The SANS Institute's *Security Awareness Tip of the Day* RSS feed [https://www.sans.org/tip_of_the_day.php]
- The SANS Institute's monthly newsletter *OUCH!* [https://www.securingthehuman.org/resources/news-letters/ouch/2015#ouch_archives]
- *CSO* magazine's quarterly newsletter *Security Smart* [http://www.securitysmartnewsletter.com/]
- *Information Week's* cybersecurity news site *Dark Reading* [http://www.darkreading.com/about-us/d/d-id/1113937]
- *The Guardian's* Information Security section [http://www.theguardian.com/media-network/information-security]
- Purdue University's Center for Education and Research in Information Assurance and Security [http://www.cerias.purdue.edu/]
- The Department of Homeland Security's Cybersecurity section [http://www.dhs.gov/topic/cybersecurity]

PART III

REIMAGINING GOVERNMENT

CHAPTER 7

DIGITAL REDESIGN:
Imagining a New Future

Why does a trip to the average motor vehicle agency feel like being transported back to the 1980s? We get agitated when Instagram takes two seconds longer than usual to load but still consider it normal to wait two hours to get a driver's license.

Technology now makes it possible to ditch a physical license in favor of a digital one stored on your smartphone. It's possible to renew your registration or driver's license online or have your insurance company perform certain transactions on your behalf. It's even possible to take your practical driver's test on a sensor-equipped electronic track without an instructor in the car.

But in most of the world, digital solutions to conduct such government business have been scattered, inconsistent, and limited in their reach and impact—if they exist at all. One agency may have an impressive mobile application but long wait times for in-person services. Another may offer great in-person service but lack digital options for those unable to physically visit the office. Doing things that you *have* to do by law—paying tickets, renewing licenses, and other mundane transactions—shouldn't be any harder than doing the things you *want* to do. But this often isn't the case.

Motor vehicle agencies are just one of the many citizen-facing areas of government that could use a thorough digital makeover. Is there a killer app for regulatory compliance? What does a best-in-class digitally enabled customer experience look like in the public sector?

Answering such questions requires fundamentally reimagining what government could look like in the digital age. This chapter expands the concept of digital transformation: going beyond delivering digital services to entirely redesigning government services and exploring new ways of achieving the mission.

By applying this book's principles and strategies—from human-centered design to leveraging disruptive technologies to engaging the broader ecosystem—government agencies can transform into digitally savvy organizations. Let's start with the area of human services, in particular, child welfare.

REDESIGNING CHILD WELFARE BY FOCUSING ON THE USER EXPERIENCE

A call comes into a child-abuse hotline, and a child protective service worker is dispatched—sometimes in a timely fashion, sometimes not. If a child is found to be in imminent danger, it's the beginning of a hopelessly fragmented, linear process involving caseworkers, the courts, health care, children's advocates, community service providers, family, friends, schools, and potentially law enforcement. Kids can get quickly lost, shuffled off to some institution, or bounced from one foster care placement to another. It's a system that's neither child- nor family-friendly, nor is it particularly hospitable to those working inside the system.

And in most jurisdictions, the confusion among key players is embedded in information technology systems. Old and outdated desktop applications require caseworkers to slog through page after page of often irrelevant questions, required checks, and input boxes. The systems are often accessible only from the office and shut out key players such as courts or service providers. Caseworkers can't access or update case files from the field, much less locate the information in a quick, intuitive manner. The IT systems are designed, it seems, to chain caseworkers to their desks and eat up their time when they could be in the field serving clients.

The same types of problems exist in other human service areas, including such large-scale programs as welfare, income assistance, and food stamps. These linear processes don't accommodate exceptions, aren't easily accessible to either workers or clients, and aren't integrated with other systems.

The inefficiency and opacity of these high-stakes, high-cost programs have for years stymied and frustrated the staff, advocates, and clients who care most about them. But the world of children and family services is on the cusp of a revolution.

In this transformed world, a new generation of web- and cloud-based IT allows for rapid access to key information about cases from virtually anywhere. Take the new child welfare system in New South Wales, Australia. Called ChildStory, it sounds like an IT system built around individual children, and that's precisely what it is.

"Really early on, we understood that naming a project 'Frontline replacement systems' was not going to talk to people, and

ChildStory was the one that stuck because what we're trying to drive through all this is a child-centered conversation," explains program co-director Lisa Alonso Love.[1]

ChildStory flips the traditional needs-based service-delivery model of social service, making the child the focus of the system and—more importantly—one of its actual users. "We're really trying to turn this whole thing on its head," says co-director Greg Wells.

For example, one of ChildStory's unique capabilities is the "digital suitcase." It's essentially a repository in which children and their caretakers collect photos, videos, documents, school reports, and other digital memorabilia. Such items are often lost as children move around within the system or leave care. "This will preserve their history, the way that our parents would do for us," Love says. The value of that virtual suitcase is enormous, both to children and to those responsible for them, and it fits neatly with ChildStory's system, allowing caseworkers to swiftly and easily track a child's relationships and support networks. It was designed with input from frontline workers—the build crew conducted 205 co-design workshops, two dozen work shadows, and close to 100 interviews.

Placing the child at the center of the system impacts how employees approach their work. "If you're writing in a system, and the child that you're writing about is going to see that information, you automatically do it in a more respectful way," Love says. The team at the New South Wales Department of Family and Community Services, and particularly those involved in developing ChildStory, hope the project will serve as an exemplar of what's possible for government. "This shows that this way of doing digital not only works, but in most cases, it delivers a better result," says Martin Stewart-Weeks, a director at the Australian Centre for Social Innovation. "I would like to think this would be the virus—spread and caught by other parts of the public service."[2]

Systems such as ChildStory illustrate how improving human services systems requires thoughtful redesign, not just better IT. The system for too long has been rooted in the view that clients—in this case, children—are incapable of or interested in accessing services or managing their own cases. Current design forces government to do all the heavy lifting. And so the major change here is one of mindset: the clear recognition that agencies are serving unique individuals who want to be and should be actively engaged.

Public officials around the world are working on similar systems for other benefits, such as food stamps and job training. These new case-management systems try to identify real needs rather than just eligibility for benefits. They free staff from walking applicants through separate, multipage paper applications for each separate program. Web-based integrated systems also have the potential to greatly simplify the process for people applying for a new program or reestablishing their eligibility for an existing one. An applicant who authorizes access to information already available in online files can turn what was once drudge work into a one-stop process.

Finally, these new systems enable governments to generate much more useful reports on how citizens use services. That allows them to more accurately track whether programs are working and better understand how to improve them.

While human services agencies are slowly dragging themselves out of bureaucratic chaos and into a more efficient digital era, higher education is rapidly transforming itself to stay competitive with aggressive digital rivals. Several public and private universities are showing how to lead in this fast-moving digital sector.

REIMAGINING HIGHER EDUCATION BY RIDING THE DISRUPTION WAVE

A landscape of digital courses and institutions is emerging at the edges of the brick-and-mortar system. Through use of the cloud, social networks, mobile computing, and big data, this new digital education model allows entrepreneurial learners to design individual paths—with completion in as little as four months—based on personal goals.

Alternative education providers such as HackReactor, a San Francisco–based "boot camp" that teaches computer programming in an immersive training environment, offer students quick ways to acquire skills sought by employers. Students learn in flipped classrooms, watching video lectures at home and solving problems in class.[3] Competency-based degrees are emerging as a popular alternative to traditional degrees that count the completion of a certain number of credit hours. Competency-based degrees are self-paced, reward prior experience, and measure learning through demonstrated proficiency.

Sensing the growing demand from students as well as the job market, many colleges and universities are choosing to ride the digital disruption wave rather than fight it. Southern New Hampshire University's College for America,[4] Georgia Institute of Technology (Georgia Tech), the Western Governors University

(WGU), and other schools are using technology to redesign how they educate students.

WGU spent nearly a decade refining its competency-based program. Students don't need to study a subject for a certain number of hours, but they do need to demonstrate they know the subject. If they pass a test, they move on to the next online module. So they study at their own pace. If their work experience prepares them for a topic, they speed through it. If they're struggling, they slow down and take their time—although a recently graduated student mentor checks in regularly to make sure they are on track.

Because students pay a set fee per semester, it's essentially an all-you-can-learn buffet. The 100 percent online, accredited institution surpasses national averages for one-year retention rates (79 percent at WGU, 73 percent nationally) and post-graduation employment (92 percent at WGU, 91 percent nationally)—for around $6,000 a year.[5]

While some institutions are trying to harness digital disruption to their advantage by leading in areas such as personalized, competency-based education, others are doing it by finding a niche and differentiating themselves. For example, Georgia Tech aims to provide the lowest-cost options in fields undergoing a rapid growth in demand. By collaborating with AT&T and Udacity, a provider of Massive Open Online Courses (MOOCs), Georgia Tech offered its first accredited online master's program in computer science for a price tag of $7,000.[6]

Some universities are also using powerful data analytics to redesign the learning journey. Arizona State University's (ASU) online tool eAdvisor has been available since 2008. It not only helps students identify courses and majors that match their goals and talents—it helps them chart a path to a degree and navigate the administrative complexities of college. The system monitors their progress and flags students at risk of poor performance: For example, a student who hopes to be an engineer but struggles to earn a C in physics or calculus may be counseled to meet with an adviser to review and potentially revise her goals or work on a plan to get back on track.[7]

To ensure that students have what it takes to achieve a degree in their desired major, ASU's system places critical and often difficult courses at the start of their education. For example, to do well in nursing, students must excel at anatomy. "By putting those courses first, you can see if a student is going to succeed in that major early," ASU provost Elizabeth Phillips told the *New York Times*.[8] The system works in conjunction with Student-360, ASU's student database, to give the university a comprehensive view of its students' progress and areas that warrant attention. Partly owing to eAdvisor, ASU's four-year graduate rate is up 20 points since 2002.[9]

The lesson from these universities for other government units is that faced with disruptive new business models that could threaten their very existence, they've chosen to adapt to digital disruption rather than fight or retreat from it. They've used the principles of carefully researched, user-focused design to serve their students' needs instead of those of administrators and professors. Amid a changing job market and skyrocketing tuition costs, students need to know their investment will generate practical benefits. These redesigns help make sure they are getting what they pay for.

Digital technology in higher education has boosted responsiveness to students, parents, businesses, and the economy, and that touches on its impact in only one sector. Another equally sweeping example is unfolding in Helsinki and other cities where innovators are ushering in a new era in personal mobility.

SMART MOBILITY: DIGITAL-AGE TRANSPORTATION BY INTEGRATING THE ECOSYSTEM

Helsinki has an audacious goal: By 2025, it plans to eliminate the need for any city resident to own a private car. The idea is to combine public and private transport providers so citizens can assemble the fastest or cheapest mode of travel. "The city's role is to enable that market to emerge," explains Sonja Heikkilä, a transportation engineer with the Helsinki government.[10]

Bus routes would be dynamic, changing based on demand at any given moment. From planning to payment, every element of the system would be accessible through mobile devices.[11] Citizens could use their phones to arrange a rideshare, an on-demand bus, an automated car, special transport for children, or traditional public transit. They could purchase "mobility packages" from private operators that would give them a host of options depending on weather, time of day, and demand.

The idea is to take a quintessentially physical transportation system designed around vehicles, roads, bridges, subways, and buses, and reverse it to revolve around digitally enabled *individual mobility*—moving each traveler from point A to point B as quickly and efficiently as possible.

Helsinki's ambitious vision reflects a much larger phenomenon: an exciting new era of smart mobility driven by groundbreaking technological innovation. Commuters no longer need to own a car to have one at their disposal. They don't have to prearrange carpools to share a ride. They don't have to wait for a ride home when rain is pouring down and there's not an empty cab in sight.

Automakers, meanwhile, are developing next-generation connected and autonomous vehicles that will improve traffic flows and safety. Yet they are no longer simply manufacturers of products—they are also investing in a wide swath of new mobility services: everything from carsharing and rental services to multimodal trip-planning apps.

In today's digital age, transportation is becoming as much about bits and bytes as it is about roads and bridges. Sensor-powered dynamic pricing, social transport apps, mobile-enabled collaborative transport models such as ridesharing and carsharing —all can help tackle traffic congestion in major urban corridors. Driverless buses and connected cars, meanwhile, are becoming viable transport options. Google's driverless cars have already driven more than 1 million miles in autonomous mode, and the company is running pilot and testing programs with small fleets of fully autonomous vehicles in Mountain View, CA, and Austin, TX.[12]

All of this change presents both opportunities and challenges for transportation departments that maintain physical infrastructure.[13] Many agencies excel at this task. But in the new world of smart transport, with its emphasis on individual behavior, flexibility, and digital apps from multiple sources, they may be called on to play a much different and much broader role.

Urban planners are trying to understand how today's digitally enabled mobility ecosystem can help advance public policy goals such as reducing congestion. These policies also could yield related benefits such as fewer traffic accidents, better air quality, and a smaller urban footprint for parking. Yet today these benefits go largely unrealized because innovative transportation business models tend to operate in silos.

What's needed is an entity that can integrate all these different transportation players and innovations. Government transportation agencies are the logical organizations to take on this challenge. In such integrator roles, they could explore partnerships that extend the reach of ridesharing companies to further the policy goals of increasing carpooling and reducing congestion. Or they could encourage carsharing as part of a long-term strategy to build greater public awareness of multimodal options.[14] They could even try to get more people to ride bikes or support research and testing of autonomous vehicles through public-private partnerships such as Mcity in Ann Arbor, MI, which provides a platform to enable automated vehicle (and feature) testing.[15]

Transportation is by no means the only public sector area that could benefit from governments functioning more as integrators of innovative, digitally enabled models and services and less as direct suppliers. In an age of exponential change, this integrator role enables agencies to tap into the latest and greatest digital innovations. That's a much better way for government to serve citizens than for it to be perpetually behind the curve, trying to replicate those innovations in-house.

RETOOLING GOVERNMENT'S OPERATING SYSTEM: OPEN, LEARNING, AND ADAPTIVE

Barcelona is thinking even bigger than Helsinki: Its goal is to become one of the world's smartest cities. Powered by Internet of Things technology, data streams through every nook and cranny of the city. Lampposts equipped with fiber-optic cables and Wi-Fi double as telecommunications towers capable of monitoring crowds, noise, weather, and traffic. Sensor-powered trash bins signal garbage trucks to empty them only when they're full. Gardeners manage irrigation of the city's green spaces using a network of sensors in the ground that transmits live data on humidity, temperature, wind velocity, sunlight, and atmospheric pressure.[16] Citizens carry their digital identity on the city's MobileID smartphone app, which allows easy access to digital public services—from registering for the census to retrieving their towed vehicles.[17]

Sensors have transformed the city's public transit systems. Interactive bus stops help riders peruse schedules and local attractions on touch-enabled digital displays. Smart parking spaces send information on vacant spots directly to drivers' smartphones. And the city's redesigned bus routes have improved efficiency and increased ridership 30 percent in four years.

"For me, the cities of the future will be like a smartphone," says Josép-Ramon Ferrer, the former director of Smart City Barcelona. "We have a lot of hardware, but it isn't anything unless it interfaces with the OS. If there are 200 platforms and 200 providers, it is a mess and not sustainable." This thinking is behind the creation of a single unified operating system to run the entire city.[18]

Barcelona isn't alone in reconceptualizing the city as a platform. The city of Bristol in the United Kingdom has partnered with the University of Bristol on a futuristic research project called Bristol Is Open. The project aims to develop a "programmable city."

Bristol has laid the hardware by building a resilient Wi-Fi mesh network on its lampposts, providing higher-speed wireless along a scenic riverside district, and running a superfast fiber-optic cable network under abandoned cable TV ducts. The city wisely bought the ducts a decade ago, and they're prepared for more upgrades—Bristol will be ready for 10G mobile broadband whenever it arrives.[19]

Dimitra Simeonidou, the CTO of Bristol Is Open, believes its OS architecture will revolutionize how citizens experience local government. "It's actually going to transform cities the same way that Android transformed the mobile phone industry," Simeonidou says. "Anybody could program and customize a service for themselves."[20] The infrastructure is technologically agnostic, enabling manufacturers to build applications on the city's open data platform.

With information from so many sensors feeding into the University of Bristol's supercomputer, it could optimize many city services. Captured data could fight traffic congestion, monitor air quality, or help the elderly live safely and independently. Crime data could be combined with surveillance and sociological models to intervene before criminal acts happen.[21]

Cities as platforms should be just a first step. What if we think bigger? Over the years, private sector companies have excelled at tracking metrics, using data analytics, and building feedback loops into their processes. Continuous iteration and improvement is the norm, not the exception. Agencies, more than most entities, could benefit from this approach.

What if we could develop a "cognitive government"—one that is itself a learning, intelligent system that adapts in concert with other systems? Emerging cognitive technologies such as machine learning, natural language processing, and artificial intelligence could augment cognitive governments. Agencies that learn from interactions with data and humans could continuously reconfigure in pursuit of better outcomes.

A cognitive operating system would involve at least three core elements:

OPEN FUNCTIONALITY

Open government and open data represent faith in the public's intelligence. But a public worth trusting with information is also a public worth collaborating with in the redesign effort. Government needs to evolve from opening up data to co-creating new solutions and models of service delivery. Government agencies that leverage the collective intelligence of the wider community can become parts of collaborative digital ecosystems.

Turning to large groups of people to solve problems, make decisions, and generate ideas for new delivery models in a decentralized way is not a new concept. However, advances in technology and societal changes have made the process of tapping the wisdom of the crowd easier and more direct.

The accessibility and affordability of social, mobile, and cloud technologies allow groups of ordinary citizens to chip away at tough societal problems by the hundreds, thousands, or even millions. This technology-enabled approach to problem solving takes many forms, including microtasking and microvolunteerism, crowdsourcing, peer-to-peer models, and prize challenges.

The rapid development of facial recognition technology at Facebook shows how a data pool of billions can produce technological change. Likewise, government agencies are learning the value of soliciting widespread citizen reactions. Deep wells of user feedback can turn beta tests into extraordinarily thorough quality-control trials. Ideas and prototypes contributed by citizens offer a wider variety of potential solutions than any team of experts can identify. Far-flung volunteers can classify data, such as identifying galaxy clusters in photographs or serving as A/B testing groups for educational software.

The SmartSantander project in the Spanish city of Santander offers a preview of the possibilities. The city-run project involves 20,000 sensors that measure traffic flow, parking spaces, noise, pollution, temperature, moisture levels, and other metrics from fixed locations such as buildings, parks, streetlights, and bus stops.[22] Santander residents can add to the information flow by downloading an app that turns their smartphones into sensors.

All the data generated through these sensors is stored in a city database.[23] City officials analyze it on a real-time basis to adjust the amount of energy they use, the number of trash pick-ups needed in a given week, and how much water to sprinkle on the lawns of city parks.[24] They have also made the information available to developers to create consumer services.

For example, SmartSantanderRA, an augmented reality mobile application, includes information on more than 2,700 beaches, parks, monuments, tourism offices, and other city sites. The user just points her smartphone to a particular building—say, a concert hall—to get a short description about events taking place there and who is performing. The app also allows real-time access to traffic flows, weather reports and forecasts, public bus information, and bike-rental services.[25]

It is not hard to imagine developers eventually using the data to create an app locating the nearest parking spot. To test it, they could roll it out to residents who have opted to turn their smart-phones into sensors and fine-tune it based on user feedback. In this way, citizens play a dual role in the SmartSantander project: They not only contribute to the data stream by turning their smartphones into sensors—they act as users of the services.

Collaborative change does not happen accidentally. As we saw in chapter 2 with the US Department of Energy's SunShot

Catalyst program, public leaders can quicken the pace of change by sparking others to develop innovative new delivery models. The White House, for example, recently invited game designers and educators to produce educational video games through a "game jam." Afterward, designers received immediate feedback from children. Not all the games will ultimately prove educational or reach completion, but a diverse array of prototypes will populate the market.

Tech companies in general, as well as game designers, are excited about the multibillion-dollar market for educational software.[26] But to create great educational software, they need to ford the "moat" between their products and the millions of students who might benefit from them. Steven Hodas, the former executive director of the Office of Innovation at the New York City Department of Education, attempted to bridge this gap by creating an educational innovation zone, or iZone. At least six states have implemented iZones, with districts releasing member schools from certain educational requirements so that they can experiment with new educational models and technology.

New York's iZone, founded in 2010, includes more than 300 schools. A typical initiative was a Gap App Challenge in which vendors competed to produce programs that might close a performance gap in middle school math; the challenge incentivized vendors by allowing them to develop relationships directly with educators.

The education innovation model that iZone fosters is not a big bang implementation initiative. As Hodas rightly says, "Innovation is not a noun; it's not a thing that I hand to you. It is a process."[27] After the success of the first Gap App Challenge, iZone worked on improving it the second time around. Using a

Gates Foundation grant, it initiated the Short-Cycle Evaluation Challenge (SCEC) to evaluate the products created during the challenge.[28]

The focus here, again, was on collaboration and a quick process of getting products from design to launch. The SCEC enabled iZone to pair educators with educational-technology developers to evaluate products based on three key criteria: for whom does the product work, when, and under what circumstances.[29]

Because lack of teacher training has hindered adoption of technology in the classroom, Gap App prototypes included teachers in the development of the apps themselves. Teachers not only saw their input appear in the programs, they could also adjust the technology to their teaching style. In this model of co-creation, designers developed technology in concert with public servants rather than imposing a rigid blueprint on users.

iZone is a good example of how microecosystems can be formed around issues—in this case, educational technology. But how can agencies scale up such pockets of innovation? By turning their data into a currency that others can use to produce new societal innovations.

This is where application programming interfaces (APIs) can help. APIs facilitate the development of third-party applications and products from government data. For instance, in 2012, the US Census Bureau released its first API, allowing developers to design web and mobile apps using its data. Using the census API, developers built sophisticated apps such as America's Economy, which provides real-time updates for 19 key economic indicators including employment, manufacturing, international trade, retail sales, and residential construction and sales.[30] APIs enable ordinary citizens to become a part of the process of digital redesign.

APPLIED LEARNING: GOVERNMENT AS A LEARNING SYSTEM

"The technology industry is evolving at a pace that the government has not kept up with," US Digital Service Administrator Mikey Dickerson said during a Yahoo News conference on tech and politics at Drake University in Iowa. "At a large scale... website design fashions are changing very quickly. People are getting much better at designing products that are intuitive and easy to use."[31]

For governments to avoid falling ever further behind the dizzying technological changes of our age would entail reinventing government as a cognitive learning system. Agencies would need to become more nimble in their ability to sense and respond. The skills to quickly prototype, test, and learn from failure would be standard requirements in nearly every project rollout. Agility, leanness, user-centricity, and design thinking would become guiding principles of governments that put learning and adapting at the center of their operating model.

"Beta government" means rapid trials and scaling to meet shifting needs and demands—small prototypes and pilots, staged rollouts, and allowance for small failures in an attempt to avert larger failures down the road. When Michael Bloomberg was elected mayor of New York City, education reform was at the top of his agenda. In addition to the iZone, his administration championed charter schools so that the city ran essentially 99 different beta versions of education reform. As new models were tested, they could be tweaked, and those that excelled could be expanded.

Testing and iteration help agencies learn, but tests need high-quality assessment, and cognitive governments need analytics.

Analytics and predictive algorithms can help identify problems that merit urgent intervention, but data alone is not enough.

Sometimes the data can identify a proper response—for instance, if an actuarial model identifies a policyholder as a risky driver, the logical next step is to increase his insurance rates. Yet predictive models often identify a risk without an obvious solution. Let's say data identified individuals likely to default on child support payments. How do you intervene? Data scientist James Guszcza considers this a "last-mile problem." Such challenges call for the marriage of analytics and behavioral science.[32] The two disciplines swirl into a virtuous feedback loop: Analytics identifies problems; insights from behavioral economics suggest targeted nudges to produce desired results; analysis of those experiments informs better science; governments refine practices based on what works.

This is the approach the state of New Mexico used to tackle a thorny problem: fraudulent unemployment insurance claims. Officials at the New Mexico Department of Workforce Solutions recognized that a large portion of fraudulent claims were the result of small fibs, not identity theft or hard fraud. So rather than taking the traditional "chase and recover" approach, they employed behavioral-economics principles to nudge claimants to be more honest.

One technique was to trigger pop-up messages at moments when people were most likely to be dishonest. Claimants were selected to see different pop-up messages at random when predictive analytics indicated a higher risk for misreporting past earnings. A dozen different messages were tested at first. Because claimants must visit the site each week to certify their eligibility, New Mexico was able to build up a large sample size quickly. In fact, a statistically significant difference was evident only three days after the system went live. After a few months, New Mexico was able to determine which messages most effectively encouraged claimants to report earnings. Overall, claimants who saw pop-up messages were 31 percent more likely to report earnings.

Additionally, each week, claimants were asked to indicate their plans for next week. With this prompting, New Mexico hopes to encourage more people to seek and therefore to find jobs.[33] By trying, testing, and tweaking new approaches, governments can be nimble and effective in solving what were once considered chronic problems.

ADAPTIVE, FLEXIBLE WORKFORCE

For governments to become more agile and adaptive organizations based on learning, they'll have to break some rules. In *The Rule of Nobody*, Philip K. Howard ably documents how bureaucracy, regulations, and dead laws tie the hands of public sector leaders and lead to sclerotic government.[34] Fixing the problem requires understanding and changing the "rules" that define the architecture of government and limit it. Examples include procurement and data sharing (discussed in chapters 4 and 5), organizational design and job descriptions, hiring and firing, and contracting. Let's take a closer look at the rules and structures governing public sector workforces.

Millennials and now generation Z, the cohort of people born after the millennials, value cutting-edge technology, flexibility, and a sense of purpose in their jobs. "This is the first generation of people that work, play, think, and learn differently than their parents.... They are the first generation to not be afraid of technology. It's like the air to them," writes Don Tapscott, author of

Grown Up Digital.[35] To hire, retain, and nurture the new generation of public-sector employees, governments need to explore ways to reinvigorate their workforce models. So how can they achieve this? What would a government workforce look like if it were redesigned for the digital age?

The GovCloud model proposed by Deloitte's GovLab represents the future of government HR: agile, efficient, truly collaborative, and designed to fit the talents and preferences of young employees as well as meet the evolving needs of government organizations. The permanent public workforce generally operates under what self-described "productive friction instigator" John Seely Brown calls the steamboat model—"fire up the engines and full steam ahead." But in Brown's analogy, millennials in today's workforce are more like kayakers zigzagging through whitewater. With this in mind, GovCloud would apply the job-hopping consultant model to the permanent workforce and use the cloud to facilitate it.[36]

Imagine a twentysomething techie—let's call her Tina—starting a job at the Department of Energy. After working at the agency for over a year, Tina finds herself seeking a new challenge. Under the GovCloud model, she could undertake a wide variety of creative, problem-focused work in a virtual staffing cloud. And she wouldn't be limited to the Department of Energy.

While these young workers may vary in background and expertise, they exhibit traits of "free agents"—self-sufficiency, self-motivation, and strong loyalty to teams, colleagues, and clients. A cloud system would allow teams to form and dissolve as needed, encouraging civil servants to focus on specific project outcomes rather than ongoing operations. Tina, for instance, could start a six-month stint at the Department of Health and Human Services helping design mobile apps for social workers. As a cloud worker, she could go wherever her skills are needed and where her passion draws her—learning and growing along the way.

Brown takes this further and envisions "a strange twist on eHarmony, in which we would use algorithms to match employees and create agile and diverse work teams where people could learn from each other. In short, the algorithms would help orchestrate serendipity."[37]

This model could also effectively allow workers to periodically refresh their skills and spread best practices from one part of the organization to the other. If the current skills gaps in government tell us anything, it's that as technology and the nature of work change, so do the skills needed to support them. Learning and re-learning has never been more important. Tracking each employee's competency through a system of experience points and badges could help translate skills and experience gained through effective work on projects, training, education, and professional certifications. It might replace the traditional tenure-centric approach.[38]

Recently, GovCloud went from being a cool concept to reality. 18F began its partnership with the Office of Personnel Management's experimental GovConnect initiative. GovConnect currently has three models of a more agile federal workforce: GovProject allows employees to apply to work on special projects for 20 percent of their workweek; GovStart encourages projects designed by employees—for example, a team of call center employees at the Department of Housing and Urban Development created a mobile app to help low-income families find affordable housing; and GovCloud allows agencies to hire workers who move between agencies and projects based on the skills required.[39] 18F researchers are exploring best practices, patterns, and pain points of successful pilots and working on the next step of GovConnect—a starter kit with techniques to help programs scale up.[40]

A more flexible staffing model such as GovConnect would appeal to younger talent and private sector workers—two types of people who have so far proven particularly critical to advancing government's digital journey.

THE CIA'S DIGITAL NERVE CENTER

With the digital agenda picking up steam across government, it's no surprise that even the security-conscious CIA is bringing its intelligence and espionage activities into the new era. The agency needed an update. Deputy Director David S. Cohen explains: "As proud as we are of the cutting-edge clandestine technology we've developed for use in the field, our officers still can't bring smartphones into work, and we've only recently figured out how to allow some personnel to take notes in a meeting on a laptop instead of with a pen and paper."[41]

In October 2015, the agency launched the Directorate of Digital Innovation (DDI)—its first new directorate in over half a century and a pioneer in the CIA's IT modernization and cyberupgrade efforts.

The DDI has three arms: a center for managing cyberthreats, a division handling IT enterprise, and an open-source center. The cyberthreats function is self-explanatory, while the IT enterprise team looks to aggressively retire legacy systems and deploy applications faster. The open-source center focuses on monitoring publicly available data such as social media feeds to understand ground realities in ways that traditional espionage misses—think Twitter during the Arab Spring.[42] It also shares information. By operating with the philosophy "all data is Agency data," the center aims to make data from different pockets of the CIA available to those who need it, thus tearing down data silos within the agency.[43]

What the DDI plans to achieve with digital goes beyond technology upgrades: The CIA wants to fully integrate digital into its culture. The agency is also focused on nurturing the next generation of digital-savvy leaders; it plans to help officers build on their digital acumen and apply it to the agency's mission and tradecraft.[44]

With the DDI's launch, the CIA has acknowledged the importance not only of being digital-ready but of constant evolution. "Any organization, whether public sector or private sector, needs to be in a process of continuous improvement and adaptation," says CIA Director John Brennan.[45]

CONCLUSION: CARVING THE PATH TO GOVERNMENT'S DIGITAL FUTURE

As governments make strides in technology, their major challenge is twofold: keeping up with the pace of change and adapting to these rapid advances. As Jack Welch famously said when he was CEO of General Electric, "If the rate of change on the outside exceeds the rate of change on the inside, the end is near."

How government bodies evolve and adapt matters to us all. In a world of exponential change, we—and they—have the potential to move more people out of poverty than ever before, to arrest or eradicate terrible disease, and to reverse the threat of global warming. But the degree to which the public sector is able to achieve these goals hinges on its capacity for continuous adaptation based on ongoing real-world experience. Can our governments become leaders in an age of exponential change?

It's a worthy challenge. To truly adapt means moving beyond the easy fix. As we saw with the FCC's technology modernization, successful digital redesigns shed legacy systems, but they do so thoughtfully and empower employees to be positive change agents. Australia's ChildStory and Transport for London's mobile program demonstrate that the best upgrades to government incorporate feedback from frontline staff, co-creation with stakeholders, and a steady focus on users. New York City's analytics squad shows how the most successful digital transformations don't just generate data and analytics—they consult experts who can explain what the data means and how to experiment with it.

The most digitally mature organizations are strong for only an instant; like 18F and the UK's GDS they never cease evolving, routinely scrapping existing procedures and adopting new ones in a permanent cycle of change and improvement. Like Access Health CT and VicRoads they avoid failure by preparing for failure—by testing, retesting and war-gaming everything that can go wrong and, in true digital fashion, they never stop iterating and improving on digital solutions. This goes doubly for cyber-defense, where standing still is a recipe for disaster. Cyber-savvy governments modify their defenses so fast that hackers waste money and time probing systems that have already changed.

Digitally mature governments also build digitally savvy workforces. They reskill their employees through digital academies like the UK's Department for Work and Pensions. They develop the next generation of cybersecurity warriors—as South Korea is doing with its mock cyber war games for teenagers. They further their digital capabilities by fostering deep engagement with the external tech community. And recognizing that procurement is a key piece of the digital transformation puzzle, they take a page from the HHS Buyers Club and US Digital Service and train a new cadre of acquisition professionals in agile contracting and other innovative purchasing techniques.

The wide reach of government lies not just in serving its citizens but, taking a cue from the US Department of Energy's SunShot Catalyst program, in making them partners in the constant reach to improve those services through technology. As governments become ever more digitally competent, they may push us into delivering on the promise of democracy. Like the Western Governors University, an exemplary digital government would serve individual citizens according to their unique needs. It would be nimble and flexible like the digital innovators from Code for America, not a bureaucracy bound in red tape. It would follow the example of Estonia and make the machinery of the system fade to the background while citizens interact, conduct business, and get on with their lives. Excellence is what citizens expect, and at this point in government's cyberdevelopment, there's no reason to deny them.

Most important to achieving government's digital future are the people who will drive the transformation. Attracting innovators with a digital mindset into government—changemakers like the ones you've met in this book—and supporting those already there is essential. Like Mike Bracken, they'll rock the boat. Like

Jim Wadleigh, they'll make people uncomfortable. Like Jen Pahlka, they'll question everything about current ways of working and challenge every assumption about how government should deliver services to citizens. But at the end of the day, the digital transformation described in this book simply won't happen without people like them. A growing cadre of digital innovators is as indispensable to achieving government's digital future as are the technologies that enable it.

CHAPTER 7 PLAYBOOK

IMAGINING A NEW FUTURE

SUCCESS STRATEGIES

Ride the disruption wave—don't avoid it. In an environment defined by constant change and frequent disruption, it's vital to not just keep up with disruptive change but to capitalize on it. On their journey to becoming more digitally transformed, some public sector organizations are focused on staying ahead of disruption instead of simply being disrupted.

Create horizon-scanning capability. Making sense of the ever-changing technology landscape can be daunting, but technology itself may provide some potential answers in the form of useful new tools. The Intelligence Advanced Research Projects Activity (IARPA), a research agency under the US director of national intelligence's responsibility, has developed automated tools to help intelligence analysts anticipate the newest technologies and innovations.[46]

Work around legacy systems. Dealing with redesign while legacy systems continue to power basic services can be a challenge for government agencies. The UK Driver and Vehicle Licensing Agency (DVLA) is adopting a "strangler approach" to tackling its legacy systems. It gets its name from strangler vines—fascinating plants that seed in the upper branches of fig trees and then work their way down until they've effectively strangled and killed the tree that was their host.[47] In similar fashion, the DVLA is gradually moving its services to a new platform—a more agile, services-based architecture—and "strangling down" pieces of the legacy platform over time. The idea is to migrate while also being able to reengineer the business processes and services but keep pushing data back to the old system, which continues to house data. When the majority of services are working on the new platform, the data can be moved over and the legacy system decommissioned.

Build partnerships and ecosystems. Whether it's smart cities or future transportation models or education innovation, partnerships and collaboration with different ecosystem players can accelerate the impact of redesign. Co-creation and collaborative efforts with universities, innovation labs, private sector organizations, or even willing citizens can help bright spots and pockets of innovation scale at a faster pace.

Flip orthodoxies. When approaching redesign, start with a clean slate and an open mind. More importantly, start with the user at the center of your redesign. Examples such as ChildStory in Australia or Helsinki's transportation plans demonstrate the power of challenging the norm.

Fail fast, fail quickly. To adapt faster to rapid advances in technology, make test-fail-learn-and-test-again a virtuous cycle in government.

TOOLS AND TECHNIQUES

Design thinking, or human-centered design. Build a deep understanding of users and their problems and then generate ideas, build prototypes and test those with users before developing and launching a service or product.

Business-model generation canvas. This downloadable tool and web app allows users to describe, design, challenge, invent, and pivot their business models. A prestructured canvas lays out the nine building blocks of any business model; users can then visualize and modify their own model in a single view using the canvas. [www.businessmodelgeneration.com/canvas/bmc]

Disruptive hypothesis. One way to unlock innovative thinking is to create a disruptive hypothesis. This often starts with asking, "What if...?" Luke Williams's *How to Craft a Disruptive Hypothesis: Be Wrong at the Start to Be Right at the End* is a short read that lays out the technique for moving past clichés and crafting disruptive hypotheses to radically reimagine things. [www. amazon.com/How-Craft-Disruptive-Hypothesis-Delivers-ebook/ dp/B004G8PR5U]

Innovation labs. Public sector innovation labs devise products and solutions to societal and public problems while providing a "safe" space for innovation, collaboration, learning, and incremental experiments to take place. These entities offer governments the ability to not only examine bigger challenges but to reframe problems in a way that advances the larger objective of redesign. [www. nesta.org.uk/blog/world-labs]

Ethnographic research. By observing target users in their natural, real-world setting, instead of an artificial environment or focus group, ethnographic research provides more authentic insights into routine user behavior. Ethnographic research uses techniques such as observation, video journals, photographs, and contextual interviews.

RESOURCES (WEBSITES, BOOKS, AND OTHER COOL STUFF)

Invention by Design: How Engineers Get From Thought to Thing by Henry Petroski discusses the problem-solving thought process of engineers.

Citizenville: How to Take the Town Square Digital and Reinvent Government by Gavin Newsom and Lisa Dickey explains how ordinary citizens can shape their government for the better.

Idealized Design: How to Dissolve Tomorrow's Crisis... Today by Russell L. Ackoff, Jason Magidson, and Herbert J. Addison talks about reverse engineering an ideal solution.

Change by Design: How Design Thinking Transforms Organizations and Inspires Innovation by Tim Brown advocates applying design thinking to the organization's transformation and innovation process.

Ten Types of Innovation: The Discipline of Building Breakthroughs by Larry Keeley, Helen Walters, Ryan Pikkel, and Brian Quinn explores patterns of innovation by analyzing more than 2,000 innovations.

Gov2020 is an interactive website, based on years of research and expert interviews, that explores the future of government. [http://government-2020.dupress.com/]

Digital Age Government is a Deloitte University Press collection of articles looking at the way the digital age is transforming government, including deeper dives into human services, higher education, law and justice, and transportation. [http://dupress.com/collection/digital-age-government/]

GovCloud outlines a model for a next-generation government-wide workforce. [http://dupress.com/articles/the-future-of-the-federal-workforce/] A corresponding video explains the concept. [http://dupress.com/articles/govcloud-and-generation-y-video/]

A microsite at GovTech, *Future Structure* is a good resource for executives trying to apply systems thinking to cities and government. [www.govtech.com/fs/]

Another good resource from the GovTech stable, the Center for Digital Government explores information technology policies and best practices at the state and local level. [www.govtech.com/cdg/]

The Open Policy Making Toolkit from Gov.uk is a practical guide to techniques for more open, effective policymaking, with several elements applicable to agencies that aspire to be learning systems. [www.gov.uk/guidance/open-policy-making-toolkit]

The Millennium Project, a think tank "on behalf of humanity," coordinates forward-looking projects, studies, and resources. [http://millennium-project.org/]

The World Economic Forum's *Future of Government Smart Toolbox* provides an overview of how technology is shaping the future of governments around the world and offers scenarios for tomorrow's public sector. [www3.weforum.org/docs/GAC/2014/WEF_GAC_FutureGovernment_SmartToolbox_Report_2014.pdf]

NOTES

INTRODUCTION

1   Adrianne Jeffries, "Only Six People Managed to Enroll in Health Insurance on HealthCare.gov's First Day," *The Verge*, November 1, 2013, www.theverge.com/2013/11/1/5054302/only-six-people-managed-to-enroll-in-health-insurance-on-healthcare/in/4623357.

2   Steven Brill, *America's Bitter Pill: Money, Politics, Backroom Deals, and the Fight to Fix Our Broken Healthcare System* (New York: Random House, 2015), p. 374.

3   Ariana Cha and Lena Sun, "What Went Wrong with HealthCare.gov," *The Washington Post*, October 24, 2013, www.washingtonpost.com/national/health-science/what-went-wrong-with-healthcaregov/2013/10/24/400e68de-3d07-11e3-b7ba-503fb5822c3e_graphic.html.

4   White House, "Remarks by the President to the Wall Street Journal CEO Council," November 19, 2013, www.whitehouse.gov/the-press-office/2013/11/19/remarks-president-wall-street-journal-ceo-council.

5   Jon Gertner, "Inside Obama's Stealth Startup," *Fast Company*, June 15, 2015, www.fastcompany.com/3046756/obama-and-his-geeks.

6   18F, "Hello, world! We are 18F," March 19, 2014, https://18f.gsa.gov/2014/03/19/hello-world-we-are-18f/.

7   Under so-called Schedule A hiring authority approved by the Office of Personnel Management, US agencies can fill digital positions at the GS-11 through GS-15 level in temporary, one-year positions. These can be renewed in one-year increments, up until September 30, 2017. The authority allows agencies to recruit for positions outside USAJobs.gov, the federal government's career site.

8   Jon Gertner, "Inside Obama's Stealth Startup."

9   "Digital Government Introduction," WhiteHouse.gov, www.whitehouse.gov/sites/default/files/omb/egov/digital-government/digital-government.html, accessed November 11, 2015.

10 Shan Li, "Amazon Overtakes Wal-Mart as Biggest Retailer," *Los Angeles Times*, July 24, 2015, http://www.latimes.com/business/la-fi-amazon-walmart-20150724-story.html.

11   Kevin Ashton, "That 'Internet of Things' Thing," *RFID Journal*, January 22, 2009, www.rfidjournal.com/articles/view?4986.

12   David Schatsky, Craig Muraskin, and Ragu Gurumurthy, "Cognitive Technologies: The Real Opportunities for Business," *Deloitte* Review 16, January 26, 2015, http://dupress.com/articles/cognitive-technologies-business-applications/?coll=12201.

13   e-Estonia, "Estonian e-Residency," https://e-estonia.com/e-residents/about/, accessed December 6, 2015.

14   "The Estonian Example," Q&A with Toomas Hendrik Ilves, *The Ripon Forum*, Volume 47, No. 1. Winter 2013, http://riponsociety.org/article/the-estonian-example-qa-with-toomas-hendrik-ilves/.

15   Julian Hattem, "President: Estonians Should Have Built HealthCare.gov," The Hill, September 3, 2014, http://thehill.com/policy/technology/216478-obama-estonians-should-have-built-healthcaregov.

16   Atmel Team, "These Smart Potholes Tweet Complaints Directly to City Officials," Bits & Pieces, June 4, 2015, http://blog.atmel.com/2015/06/04/these-potholes-are-tweeting-complaints-directly-to-city-officials/.

17   Kyle Wiggers, "Google Patents a System for Cars that Maps Potholes," August 25, 2015, *Digital Trends*, www.digitaltrends.com/android/google-pothole-detection/.

18   Benjamin Zhang, "Google Wants to Use Technology to Get Rid of Potholes," Business Insider, September 1, 2015, http://www.businessinsider.com/google-has-patented-a-way-to-hunt-down-potholes-2015-8.

19   National Association of State Chief Information Officers, "CIOs Make a Difference," http://new.nascio.org/CIOsMakeaDifference/CIOTwo.html, accessed December 7, 2015.

20   Jon Raphael, "How Artificial Intelligence Can Boost Audit Quality," *CFO*, June 2015, ww2.cfo.com/auditing/2015/06/artificial-intelligence-can-boost-audit-quality/.

21   Albuquerque, NM, "Smart Policing," March 1, 2013, www.smartpolicinginitiative.com/SPIsites/albuquerque-nm.

22   Tatiana Schlossberg, "New York Police Begin Using ShotSpotter System to Detect Gunshots," *The New York Times*, March 16, 2015, www.nytimes.com/2015/03/17/nyregion/shotspotter-detection-system-pinpoints-gunshot-locations-and-sends-data-to-the-police.html.

23   In the United States, millennials lead in the Internet usage category, with 93 percent going online regularly, but they are matched by the gen Xers (89 percent) in the category. Understandably, baby boomers use the Internet less than the other two, but even then nearly 80 percent from the generation are regular Internet users. Source: "How Digital Behavior Differs among Millennials, Gen Xers and Boomers," *eMarketer*, March 21, 2013, www.emarketer.com/Article/How-Digital-Behavior-Differs-Among-Millennials-Gen-Xers-Boomers/1009748.

24   William D. Eggers and Joel Bellman, *The Journey to Digital Transformation*,
      Deloitte University Press, October 2, 2015, http://dupress.com/articles/digital-
      transformation-in-government/.
25   Greg Godbout and Noah Kunin, "Hacking Bureaucracy: Improving Hiring
      and Software Deployment," 18F, May 5, 2014, https://18f.gsa.gov/2014/05/14/
      hacking-bureaucracy-improving-hiring-and-software/.

CHAPTER 1

1   "Speech by BIS Permanent Secretary Martin Donnelly," Institute for Government,
      June 30, 2014, http://www.instituteforgovernment.org.uk/news/latest/speech-
      bis-permanent-secretary-martin-donnelly.
2   Institute for Government, "Digital Government: The Strategy is Delivery—Mike
      Bracken, Head of the Government Digital Service," October 20, 2014, http://
      www.instituteforgovernment.org.uk/events/digital-government-strategy-
      delivery-mike-bracken-head-government-digital-service-1.
3   Telephone interview with Mike Bracken, August 10, 2015.
4   Mike Bracken, "From Policy to Delivery: Changing the Organising Principle
      of the Civil Service," Speech to the Institute for Government, October 21,
      2014, http://mikebracken.com/blog/on-policy-and-delivery/.
5   Constantijn van Oranje-Nassau, speech at the Deloitte Global Public Sector
      Leadership meeting, Amsterdam, Netherlands, June 8, 2015.
6   United Nations Public Administration Network, "The Global e-Government
      Forum 2013 Kicks off in S. Korea," October 22, 2013, http://www.unpan.org/
      PublicAdministrationNews/tabid/651/mctl/ArticleView/ModuleID/1555/
      articleId/39376/Default.aspx.
7   Interview with Eric Mill, Washington, DC, April 17, 2015.
8   Forrester Research Inc., *Washington Must Work Harder to Spur the Public's
      Interest in Digital Government*, by Rick Parrish, Harley Manning, and Carla
      O'Connor, April 28, 2015, https://www.forrester.com/Washington+Must+
      Work+Harder+To+Spur+The+Publics+Interest+In+Digital+Government/
      fulltext/-/E-RES115905?aid=AST1002746#AST1002746.
9   Interview with Kathy Settle, London, UK, March 4, 2014.
10   Interview with Greg Godbout, Washington, DC, October 16, 2014.
11   Interview with Jennifer Pahlka, San Francisco, CA, January 29, 2015.
12   Deloitte, *Comparative Study of the Personal Income Tax Return Process: In
      Belgium and 33 Other Countries*, 2nd ed., May 2013, http://www2.deloitte.
      com/content/dam/Deloitte/be/Documents/tax/TaxStudiesAndSurveys/
      Personal%20income%20tax%20return%20study_EN_2013.pdf.

13 See, for instance, Fraser Institute, *Prefilled Personal Income Tax Returns: A Comparative Analysis of Australia, Belgium, California, Quebec, and Spain*, Francois Vaillancourt, ed., June 2011, http://www.fraserinstitute.org/sites/default/files/prefilled-personal-income-tax-returns.pdf.

14 Bracken interview, August 10, 2015.

15 Michael E. Porter, *Competitive Advantage: Creating and Sustaining Superior Performance* (New York: The Free Press, 1985), pp. 11–15.

16 Alvin Toffler, *The Third Wave* (New York: Bantam Books, 1980).

17 Philip Kotler, "The Prosumer Movement: A New Challenge for Marketers," *Advances in Consumer Research*, Volume 13, 1986, pp. 510–513, http://acrwebsite.org/volumes/6542/volumes/v13/NA-13.

18 Todd Wasserman, "4 Reasons Google Bought Waze," *Mashable*, June 11, 2013, http://mashable.com/2013/06/11/5-reasons-google-waze/.

19 United Nations Public Administration Network, "The Global e-Government Forum 2013 Kicks off in S. Korea," October 22, 2013, http://www.unpan.org/PublicAdministrationNews/tabid/651/mctl/ArticleView/ModuleID/1555/articleId/39376/Default.aspx.

20 Kaleb Francis, "Five Trends Affecting Your Market Right Now," *Idealog*, July 4, 2012, http://www.idealog.co.nz/blog/2012/07/five-trends-affecting-your-market-right-now.

21 Massachusetts Bay Transportation Authority, "App Showcase," http://www.mbta.com/rider_tools/apps/.

22 TED, "Coding a Better Government," February 2012, http://www.ted.com/talks/jennifer_pahlka_coding_a_better_government?language=en.

23 Mike Bracken, "From Policy to Delivery: Changing the Organising Principle of the Civil Service."

24 Interview with Shashank Khandelwal, Washington, DC, March 19, 2015.

25 Bracken interview, August 10, 2015.

26 William D. Eggers and John O'Leary, *If We Can Put a Man on the Moon: Getting Big Things Done in Government* (Cambridge, MA: Harvard Business Press 2009), p. 145.

27 Jill Krasny, "Malcolm Gladwell on What Really Makes People Disruptive," *Inc.*, October 7, 2014, http://www.inc.com/jill-krasny/malcolm-gladwell-on-the-one-character-trait-that-makes-people-disruptive.html?cid=ps002ros.

28 Bracken interview, August 10, 2015.

CHAPTER 2

1 Matthew Burton, "Lessons Learned from My Time at the CFPB," *O'Reilly Radar*, January 10, 2014, http://radar.oreilly.com/2014/01/lessons-learned-from-my-time-at-the-cfpb.html.

2   Ibid.

3   Megan McArdle, "Why Obama's 'iPod Presidency' Was Doomed,"
      BloombergView, November 1, 2013, http://www.bloombergview.com/
      articles/2013-11-01/why-obama-s-ipod-presidency-was-doomed.

4   Interview with Merici Vinton, London, UK, July 12, 2015.

5   Vinton interview, July 12, 2015; and Merici Vinton, "9 Things You Should Know
      Before Debating HealthCare.gov, from Someone Who Actually Launched a
      Successful Government Website," *TechPresident*, October 24, 2013, http://
      techpresident.com/news/24451/9-things-you-should-know-debating-
      healthcaregov-someone-who-actually-launched-successful.

6   Suzy Khimm, "Who Leaves Comedy Central to Work for the Government?"
      The Washington Post, September 7, 2012, http://www.washingtonpost.com/
      blogs/wonkblog/wp/2012/09/07/who-leaves-comedy-central-to-work-for-
      the-government/.

7   Ibid.

8   Vinton, "9 Things You Should Know Before Debating HealthCare.gov, from
      Someone Who Actually Launched a Successful Government Website."

9   Interview with former senior official, London, UK, March 2015.

10   United Kingdom, *The Civil Services Reform Plan*, June 2012, https://www.gov
      .uk/government/uploads/system/uploads/attachment_data/file/305148/Civil-
      Service-Reform-Plan-final.pdf.

11   Danny Palmer, "'A Modern Equivalent to London's Victorian Sewers'—
      Francis Maude Hails Importance of Government Digital Reforms," *Computing*,
      March 4, 2015, http://www.computing.co.uk/ctg/news/2398080/a-modern-
      equivalent-to-londons-victorian-sewers-francis-maude-hails-importance-
      of-government-digital-reforms.

12   United Kingdom Cabinet Office, *2010 to 2015 Government Policy: Civil Service
      Reform*, May 8, 2015, https://www.gov.uk/government/publications/2010-
      to-2015-government-policy-civil-service-reform/2010-to-2015-government-
      policy-civil-service-reform.

13   Interview with Francis Maude, Washington, DC, October 20, 2014.

14   Interview with Kathy Settle, London, UK, March 16, 2015.

15   Mike Bracken, "On Becoming Executive Director of Digital in the Cabinet
      Office," *Mike Bracken Blog*, May 20, 2011, http://mikebracken.com/blog/
      gov-uk/on-becoming-executive-director-of-digital-in-the-cabinet-office/.

16   US Digital Service, "Mikey Dickerson to SXSW: Why We Need You in Government,"
      March 26, 2015, https://medium.com/@USDigitalService/mikey-dickerson-to-
      sxsw-why-we-need-you-in-government-f31dab3263a0.

17   Iain Thomson, "Obama's HealthCare.gov Savior Says: 'No Suits Please, We're
      Techies,'" *The Register*, August 21, 2014, http://www.theregister.co.uk/2014/08/
      21/obamas_new_national_it_admin_says_no_suits_please_were_techies/.

18   Jon Gertner, "Inside Obama's Stealth Startup."

19   Ibid.

20   Ibid.

21   Godbout interview, October 16, 2014.

22   Daniel H. Pink, *Drive: The Surprising Truth About What Motivates Us* (New York: Riverhead Books), 2009.

23   Interview with Jay Nath, San Francisco, CA, July 24, 2015

24   Deloitte, *Mind the Gaps: The 2015 Deloitte Millennial Survey*, 2015, http://www2.deloitte.com/content/dam/Deloitte/global/Documents/About-Deloitte/gx-wef-2015-millennial-survey-executivesummary.pdf.

25   Godbout interview, October 16, 2014.

26   Dan Pink, *Drive*, p. 207.

27   Interview with Chris Cruz, Sacramento, CA, February 4, 2015.

28   Interview with Jennifer Tress, Washington, DC, March 10, 2015.

29   Interview with Fiona Dean, London, UK, February 3, 2015.

30   Troy K. Schneider, "More Personnel Changes at GSA," *FCW*, March 11, 2015, http://fcw.com/blogs/fcw-insider/2015/03/gsa-staff-shuffles.aspx.

31   Interview with Greg Godbout, Washington, DC, March 10, 2015.

32   Winnie Agbonlahor, "Interview: Kevin Cunnington," *CSW*, May 12, 2014, http://www.civilserviceworld.com/articles/interview/interview-kevin-cunnington.

33   Interview with Kevin Cunnington, London, UK, March 4, 2014.

34   Interview with Rick Stock, London, UK, March 4, 2014.

35   Andrew Besford, "Transformation Is a Team Sport: The Key Messages from Sprint DWP in Manchester," *Medium*, November 18, 2015, https://medium.com/@andrewbesford/transformation-is-a-team-sport-the-key-messages-from-sprintdwp-in-manchester-32cfa7c42e6d#.i6yp4w8mw.

36   "Joy's Law (Management)," *Wikipedia*, https://en.wikipedia.org/wiki/Joy's_Law_(management).

37   Barry Friedman, Kristen Ardani, David Feldman, Ryan Citron, Robert Margolis, and Jarett Zuboy, "Benchmarking Non-Hardware Balance-of-System (Soft) Costs for US Photovoltaic Systems, Using a Bottom-Up Approach and Installer Survey—Second Edition," Technical Report NREL/TP-6A20-60412, National Renewable Energy Laboratory, US Department of Energy, October 2013, http://www.nrel.gov/docs/fy14osti/60412.pdf.

38   Ibid.

39   Ibid.

40   Katherine Ryan & Abed Ali, "The New Government Leader: Mobilizing Agile Public Leadership in Disruptive Times," Deloitte University Press, August 12, 2013, http://dupress.com/articles/the-new-government-leader-mobilizing-agile-public-leadership-in-disruptive-times/.

41   Interview with Mark Schwartz, Washington, DC, July 2, 2015.

42   https://www.whitehouse.gov/digital/united-states-digital-service.

CHAPTER 3

1   A total of 14 states and DC fully operate state-run exchanges or marketplaces. Two additional states are approved as state-based.

2   Sarah Kliff, "An Interview with HealthCare.gov's New Chief Executive," *Vox*, August 26, 2014, www.vox.com/2014/6/8/5789350/how-connecticut-built-a-healthcare-gov-that-actually-works.

3   Telephone interview with Newton Wong, December 9, 2015.

4   Telephone interview with Jim Wadleigh, December 22, 2015.

5   Jeff Cohen, "Connecticut Looks to Sell Its Obamacare Exchange to Other States," *NPR*, February 28, 2014, www.npr.org/sections/health-shots/2014/02/27/283526215/connecticut-looks-to-sell-its-obamacare-exchange-to-other-states.

6   Arielle Levin Becker, "Obamacare Insurance Enrollment Begins as Officials Warn of Potential Glitches," *CT Mirror*, October 1, 2013, http://ctmirror.org/2013/10/01/obamacare-insurance-enrollment-begins-officials-warn-potential-glitches/.

7   Josie Ensor, "Sun Screen Erected Outside Walkie Talkie Tower to Block Burning Rays," *The Telegraph*, September 4, 2013, www.telegraph.co.uk/news/uknews/10285610/Sun-screen-erected-outside-Walkie-Talkie-tower-to-block-burning-rays.html.

8   Interview with Hillary Hartley, San Francisco, CA, February 20, 2015.

9   Government of the United Kingdom, "Government Digital Service Design Principles," www.gov.uk/design-principles.

10 Interview with Kathy Settle, London, UK, March 4, 2015.

11 Interview with Mark Waks, Washington, DC, April 13, 2015.

12 Interview with Deborah Stone-Wulf conducted by Greg Pellegrino for Deloitte DBriefs, "Customer Experience in the Public Sector: Making the Leap from Good to Great," November 5, 2015.

13 Transport for London, "Fit for the Future," https://tfl.gov.uk/cdn/static/cms/documents/fit-for-the-future.pdf.

14 Interview with Conor Maguire, London, UK, July 8, 2015.

15 According to the Standish Group, 29 percent of all waterfall development projects fail, compared to only 9 percent of projects using the agile methodology. See: *Chaos Report 2015*, Standish Group, p. 7, http://blog.standishgroup.com/post/50.

16 Interview with Alastair Montgomery, London, UK, July 8, 2015.

17 VersionOne Inc., "9th Annual State of Agile Survey," 2015, www.versionone.com/pdf/state-of-agile-development-survey-ninth.pdf.

18 William D. Eggers and John O'Leary, *If We Can Put a Man on the Moon: Getting Big Things Done in Government* (Cambridge, MA: Harvard Business Press, 2009), chapter 2.

19   Chip Heath and Dan Heath, *Switch: How to Change Things When Change Is Hard* (New York: Broadway Books, 2010).

20   William D. Eggers and Chip Heath, "The Secret to Successful Change," *Governing*, November 10, 2010, www.governing.com/columns/mgmt-insights/secret-successful-organization-change.html.

21   Emily Webber, "Best Agile Training? Just Do It!" *Digital Transformation Blog*, August 11, 2014, https://digitaltransformation.blog.gov.uk/2014/08/11/best-agile-training-just-do-it/.

22   Eric Bristow and Azunna Anyanwu, "9 Myths About Agile," *CIO Journal*, March 25, 2014, http://deloitte.wsj.com/cio/2014/03/25/9-myths-about-agile/.

23   Montgomery interview, July 8, 2015.

24   "V.A.-Men: Delays of Future Past," *The Daily Show*, July 10, 2014, http://thedailyshow.cc.com/videos/r9nm2k/v-a--men--delays-of-future-past.

25   US Veterans Administration, Veterans Health Administration, *Review of Alleged Patient Deaths, Patient Wait Times, and Scheduling Practices at the Phoenix VA Health Care System*, August 26, 2014, www.va.gov/oig/pubs/VAOIG-14-02603-267.pdf.

26   Gregg Zoroya, "Report: VA Scandal Probe Targets Potential Obstruction of Justice," *USA Today*, August 26, 2014, www.usatoday.com/story/news/nation/2014/08/26/va-veterans-affairs-scandal-mcdonald-phoenix/14620397/.

27   Neil Versel, "VA Scheduling Scandal Obscures System's Healthcare Quality, Interoperability Gains," *Forbes*, June 19, 2014, www.forbes.com/sites/neilversel/2014/06/19/va-scheduling-scandal-obscures-systems-healthcare-quality-interoperability-gains/.

28   US Veterans Administration, Veterans Health Administration, *Review of Alleged Patient Deaths, Patient Wait Times, and Scheduling Practices at the Phoenix VA Health Care System*, p. 73.

29   US Veterans Administration, Vets.gov Playbook, https://www.vets.gov/playbook/.

30   US Veterans Administration, "Remarks by Secretary Robert A. McDonald," Institute of Medicine Annual Meeting, Washington, DC, October 20, 2014, www.va.gov/opa/bios/secretary.asp.

31   US Veterans Administration, Vets.gov Playbook.

32   Robert McDonald, "Help Us Create Vets.gov: A Message from Secretary Robert McDonald," Vets.gov, November 11, 2015, https://www.vets.gov/2015/11/11/why-we-are-designing-in-beta.html.

33   Billy Mitchell, "Megan Smith Bullish on Digital Government," *FedScoop*, January 27, 2015, http://fedscoop.com/megan-smith-focuses-in-on-digital-government.

34   Camille Tuutti, "Service Call," *Government Executive*, March/April 2015, www.govexec.com/feature/service-call/.

35   Jason Shueh, "GSA Innovates Services with Chief Customer Officer," *Government Technology*, April 1, 2015, www.govtech.com/federal/GSA-Innovates-Services-with-Chief-Customer-Officer.html.

36   Tuutti, "Service Call."

37   Bianca Spinosa, "Can Phaedra Chrousos Move the Needle at GSA?" *FCW*, August 11, 2015, https://fcw.com/Articles/2015/08/11/Phaedra-Chrousos-profile.aspx?p=1.

38   Phaedra Chrousos, "Walking in Our Customers' Shoes," *DigitalGov*, January 16, 2015, www.digitalgov.gov/2015/01/16/walking-in-our-customers-shoes/.

39   Rick Parrish, "More US Federal Agencies Are Considering Chief Customer Officers," *1to1 Media*, February 27, 2015, www.1to1media.com/weblog/2015/02/more_us_federal_agencies_are_c.html.

40   Ripon Civic Society, "The Right Direction for Desire Lines," *Ripon Gazette*, October 10, 2013, www.riponcivicsociety.org.uk/viewoldcomment.php?ID=371&PHPSESSID=1010ojq5kmir7jqoets1v0p7p3.

41   Matthew Hancock, "National Digital Conference 2015: Keynote Speech," Gov.uk, June 25, 2015, www.gov.uk/government/speeches/national-digital-conference-2015-keynote-speech.

42   Jonathan Messinger, "Government Procurement Gets Its 'Yelp,'" *Public Spend Forum*, April 14, 2015, http://publicspendforum.net/government-procurement-gets-its-yelp/.

43   Deloitte Digital Experience, "VicRoads," November 25, 2015, www.youtube.com/watch?v=-7iSp_kYJzE.

44   Richard Perdriau and Jolanda Zerbst, "VicRoads Case Study: Bigger, Better and Responsive," UX Australia 2014, https://speakerdeck.com/richardp321/vicroads-website-case-study-bigger-better-and-responsive.

45   Ibid.

46   Telephone interview with Jason Hutchinson, December 9, 2015.

47   Deloitte Digital Experience, "VicRoads."

48   See, for instance, Andrew Reeson and Simon Dunstall, *Behavioral Economics and Complex Decision-Making: Implications for the Australian Tax and Transfer System, Commonwealth Scientific and Industrial Research Organisation*, August 7, 2009, www.taxreview.treasury.gov.au/content/html/commissioned_work/downloads/CSIRO_AFTS_Behavioural_economics_paper.pdf.

49   Tom Loosemore, "Organ Donation and A/B Testing," *Government Digital Service Blog*, August 6, 2013, https://gds.blog.gov.uk/2013/08/06/organ-donation-and-ab-testing/.

50   Hannah Moss, "Engaging Citizens in Your Digital Services," *GovLoop*, March 19, 2015, www.govloop.com/engaging-citizens-digital-services/.

51 AltSchool, "About Us," https://www.altschool.com/about-us#about-us.
52 Katrina Schwartz, "The One Room Schoolhouse Goes High Tech," *Mind/ Shift*, April 17, 2014, http://blogs.kqed.org/mindshift/2014/04/the-one-room-schoolhouse-goes-high-tech/.

CHAPTER 4

1   Schwartz interview, July 2, 2015.
2   Paul Krill, "Devops, Agile Development Cut Through Federal Agency's Red Tape," *InfoWorld*, October 23, 2014, http://www.infoworld.com/article/2837893/devops/devops-agile-development-cut-through-federal-agencys-red-tape.html.
3   Clay Johnson and Harper Reed, "Why the Government Never Gets Tech Right: Getting to the Bottom of HealthCare.gov's Flop," *The New York Times*, October 24, 2013, http://www.nytimes.com/2013/10/25/opinion/getting-to-the-bottom-of-healthcaregovs-flop.html?_r=0.
4   "Chaos 2015," The Standish Group, http://blog.standishgroup.com/post/50.
5   Interview with Mark Naggar, Washington, DC, July 2, 2015.
6   Angie Petty, "HHS Is a Major Player in the Move Toward Agile Acquisition," *GovWin*, April 28, 2015, https://iq.govwin.com/index.cfm?fractal=blogTool.dsp.blog&blogname=public&alias=HHS-is-a-Major-Player-in-the-Move-toward-Agile-Acquisition.
7   Krill, "Devops, Agile Development Cut Through Federal Agency's Red Tape."
8   Josh Russell, "A Supplier Framework for Building Digital Services," *Government Digital Service*, November 15, 2013, https://gds.blog.gov.uk/2013/11/15/a-supplier-framework-for-building-digital-services/.
9   Naggar interview, July 2, 2015.
10 Ibid.
11 HHS Idea Lab, "Mark Naggar, Project Manager," http://www.hhs.gov/idealab/staff-item/mark-naggar/, accessed December 2, 2015.
12 Mary-Louise Hoffman, "Mark Naggar: HHS Pushes 'Agile' IT Procurement Model Shift," *Executive Gov*, April 21, 2015, http://www.executivegov.com/2015/04/mark-naggar-hhs-pushes-agile-it-procurement-model-shift/.
13 Dan Ward, "Don't Come to the Dark Side: Acquisition Lessons From a Galaxy Far, Far Away," October 2011, http://www.thedanward.com/resources/Build+Droids+Not+Death+Stars.pdf.
14 Schwartz interview, July 2, 2015.
15 Ibid.
16 Ibid.

17   Ezra Klein and Evan Soltas, "Wonkbook: 11 Facts about America's Prison Population," *The Washington Post*, August 13, 2013, http://www.washingtonpost.com/news/wonkblog/wp/2013/08/13/wonkbook-11-facts-about-americas-prison-population/.

18   Anya Kamenetz, *DIY U: Edupunks, Edupreneurs, and the Coming Transformation of Higher Education* (Vermont: Chelsea Green Publishing, 2010), p. 92.

19   Carol A. Twigg, "Improving Learning and Reducing Costs: New Models for Online Learning," National Center for Academic Transformation, http://www.thencat.org/Articles/NewModels.html, accessed December 2, 2015.

20   Clayton M. Christensen and Henry J. Eyring, *The Innovative University: Changing the DNA of Higher Education From the Inside Out* (San Francisco: Jossey-Bass, 2011), p. 215.

21   Lawrence H. Dubois, *DARPA's Approach to Innovation and Its Reflection in Industry*, National Center for Biotechnology Information, 2003, http://www.ncbi.nlm.nih.gov/books/NBK36337/.

22   Fuel Cells, "Types of Fuel Cells," http://www.fuelcells.org/base.cgim?template=types_of_fuel_cells, accessed December 2, 2015.

23   Federal Bureau of Investigation, *Preliminary Annual Uniform Crime Report, January-December, 2012*, https://www.fbi.gov/about-us/cjis/ucr/crime-in-the-u.s/2012/preliminary-annual-uniform-crime-report-january-december-2012.

24   William D. Eggers and Anesa Parker, "Government Problems and the Power of Prizes," *Governing.com,* August 6, 2014, http://www.governing.com/columns/smart-mgmt/col-government-incentive-prize-competitions-problem-solving.html.

25   Interview with Jenn Gustetic, Washington, DC, December 4, 2015.

26   Jesse Goldhammer, et al., *The Craft of Incentive Prize Design: Lessons From the Public Sector*, Deloitte University Press, June 18, 2014, http://dupress.com/articles/the-craft-of-incentive-prize-design/.

27   William D. Eggers and Joel Bellman, "The Journey to Government's Digital Transformation," Deloitte University Press, October 2, 2015, http://dupress.com/articles/digital-transformation-in-government/.

28   Interview with Joanie Newhart and Traci Walker, Washington, DC, October 2, 2015.

29   Petty, "HHS Is a Major Player in the Move Toward Agile Acquisition."

30   Mark Naggar, "Unhappy with the Results of Your IT Service Acquisitions? We Heard You! / Recap Part 1," US Department of Health and Human Services, February 23, 2015, http://www.hhs.gov/idealab/2015/02/23/unhappy-results-service-acquisitions-heard-recap-part-1/.

CHAPTER 5

1   The White House, *Federal Enterprise Architecture Framework: Version 2*, January 29, 2013, www.whitehouse.gov/sites/default/files/omb/assets/egov_docs/fea_v2.pdf.

2   Paul Strassmann, "A Brief History of the Federal Enterprise Architecture," *Strassmann's Blog*, February 15, 2012, http://pstrassmann.blogspot.in/2012/02/brief-history-of-federal-enterprise.html.

3   Jason Miller, "Forman Calls for New Approach to the Federal Enterprise Architecture," *GCN*, May 20, 2004, http://gcn.com/Articles/2004/05/20/Forman-calls-for-new-approach-to-the-Federal-Enterprise-Architecture.aspx?p=1.

4   Interview with Tony Summerlin, Washington, DC, July 16, 2015.

5   Interview with Mark Forman, Salt Lake City, UT, October 16, 2015.

6   Donald Kettl, "The Next Government," *The IBM Center for the Business of Government*, November 25, 2008, www.businessofgovernment.org/blog/presidential-transition/next-government-donald-kettl.

7   Mark Thompson, "What Is Government as a Platform and How Do We Achieve It?" *Computer Weekly*, February 2015, www.computerweekly.com/opinion/What-is-government-as-a-platform-and-how-do-we-achieve-it.

8   Sean Gallagher, "De-dupe Time: GAO Finds $321 Million in Redundant Government IT Spending," *Ars Technica*, September 17, 2013, http://arstechnica.com/information-technology/2013/09/de-dupe-time-gao-finds-321-million-in-redundant-government-it-spending/.

9   Telephone interview with Mike Bracken, August 20, 2015.

10 Thompson, "What Is Government as a Platform and How Do We Achieve It?"

11 Government of the United Kingdom, "Cabinet Office Unveils Technology Transformation," February 4, 2015, www.gov.uk/government/news/cabinet-office-unveils-technology-transformation.

12 Telephone interview with Chris Atkins, October 16, 2015.

13 Jessica Hughes, "Data Analytics Helps Indiana Change Its Approach to Infant Mortality," *Government Technology*, February 3, 2015, www.govtech.com/data/Data-Analytics-Helps-Indiana-Change-its-Approach-to-Infant-Mortality.html.

14 Andrea Muraskin, "Indiana Provides $13.5 Million to Reduce Infant Mortality and Close Race Gap," *Side Effects Public Media*, May 19, 2015, http://sideeffectspublicmedia.org/post/indiana-provides-135-million-reduce-infant-mortality-and-close-race-gap.

15 Policy Exchange, "The Future of Digital Government: What's Worked? What's Not? What's Next?" June 29, 2015, www.policyexchange.org.uk/modevents/item/the-future-of-digital-government-what-s-worked-what-s-not-what-s-next.

16 Interview with David Bray, Washington, DC, May 4, 2015.

17   Aaron Boyd, "FCC CIO Leads an IT 'Intervention': David Bray Wants to Move the FCC Into the Cloud on a Grand Scale," *Federal Times*, May 14, 2015, www.federaltimes.com/story/government/interview/one-one/2015/05/14/fcc-cio-leads-intervention/27255053/.

18   Bray interview, May 4, 2015.

19   Greg Otto, "Inside the FCC's Risky IT Overhaul," *FedScoop*, January 5, 2015, http://fedscoop.com/david-bray-fcc-it-overhaul.

20   In two separate instances, a subset of commenters discovered ways to tie up the availability of the old system so that other posters could not file comments. The FCC could not block such behaviors and at the same time was limited by a 32-bit system running on on-premise hardware.

21   Bray interview, May 4, 2015.

22   Interview with David Bray, Washington, DC, October 8, 2015.

23   Instead of an estimated $3.2 million for an on-premise solution, the cloud-based solution cost the FCC only $450,000. Moreover, the costs of maintaining a cloud-based solution are only $100,000 a year versus $620,000 for an on-premise one, saving another $2.6 million over five years in upkeep.

24   Otto, "Inside the FCC's Risky IT Overhaul."

25   Bray interview, May 4, 2015.

26   Thompson, "What Is Government as a Platform and How Do We Achieve It?"

27   Otto, "Inside the FCC's risky IT overhaul."

28   Melody Kramer, "New Federalist Platform Lets Agencies Quickly Launch Websites," 18F, September 15, 2015, https://18f.gsa.gov/2015/09/15/federalist-platform-launch/.

29   Bracken interview, August 10, 2015.

30   Brett Johnson, "Working for the Cabinet Office Digital and Technology Team," *Cabinet Office Technology*, August 10, 2015, https://cabinetofficetechnology.blog.gov.uk/2015/08/10/working-for-the-cabinet-office-digital-and-technology-team/.

31   Magnus Falk, "Common Technology Services: Technology Is a Tool, Not a Barrier," *Government Digital Service*, August 25, 2015, https://gds.blog.gov.uk/2015/08/25/common-technology-services-technology-is-a-tool-not-a-barrier/.

32   Kia Gregory, "New York Tries to Rid Its Sewers of FOG (Fat, Oil, and Grease)," *The New York Times*, February 14, 2014, www.nytimes.com/2014/02/15/nyregion/new-york-tries-to-clear-its-sewers-of-fog-fat-oil-and-grease.html.

33   Gillian Tett, "Why Grease Is the Word in New York," *FT Magazine*, April 1, 2013, www.ft.com/intl/cms/s/2/a284331a-9751-11e2-a77c-00144feabdc0.html.

34   Alan Feuer, "The Mayor's Geek Squad," *The New York Times*, March 23, 2013, www.nytimes.com/2013/03/24/nyregion/mayor-bloombergs-geek-squad.html.

35   Stephen Goldsmith and Susan Crawford, *The Responsive City: Engaging Communities Through Data-Smart Governance* (San Francisco: Jossey-Bass, 2014), p. 120.

36   Interview with Michael Flowers, Washington, DC, December 11, 2014.

37   Michael Flowers, *Beyond Transparency—2013 Code for America*, Chapter 15, "Beyond Open Data: The Data-Driven City," http://beyondtransparency.org/chapters/part-4/beyond-open-data-the-data-driven-city/.

38   Alex Howard, "Predictive Data Analytics Is Saving Lives and Taxpayer Dollars in New York City," *O'Reilly Radar*, June 26, 2012, http://radar.oreilly.com/2012/06/predictive-data-analytics-big-data-nyc.html.

39   Flowers interview, December 11, 2014.

40   Viktor Schönberger and Kenneth Cukier, "Big Data in the Big Apple," *Slate*, March 6, 2013, www.slate.com/articles/technology/future_tense/2013/03/big_data_excerpt_how_mike_flowers_revolutionized_new_york_s_building_inspections.html.

41   Flowers interview, December 11, 2014.

42   "June Marks First Month Since 1916 With No Fire Deaths in NYC," Associated Press, http://pix11.com/2015/07/02/june-marks-first-month-since-1916-with-no-fire-deaths-in-nyc/.

43   City of New Orleans, "Analytics-Informed Smoke Alarm Outreach Program," March 31, 2015, http://nola.gov/performance-and-accountability/nolalytics/files/full-report-on-analytics-informed-smoke-alarm-outr/.

44   Charles Chieppo, "Where There's Smoke, There's Data," *Governing*, April 16, 2015, www.governing.com/blogs/bfc/col-new-orleans-data-analytics-targeted-smoke-alarm-outreach.html.

45   Jason Shueh, "3 Reasons Chicago's Analytics Could Be Coming to Your City," *Government Technology*, April 1, 2014, www.govtech.com/data/3-Reasons-Chicagos-Analytics-Could-be-Coming-to-Your-City.html.

46   Ash Center Mayor's Research Team, "Chicago's SmartData Platform: Pioneering Open Source Municipal Analytics," Data Smart City Solutions, January 8, 2014, http://datasmart.ash.harvard.edu/news/article/chicago-mayors-challenge-367.

47   Estonian ICT Export Cluster, "What Is e-Residency?" https://e-estonia.com/e-residents/about/.

48   Stem Tamkivi, "Lessons From the World's Most Tech-Savvy Government," *The Atlantic*, January 24, 2014, http://www.theatlantic.com/international/archive/2014/01/lessons-from-the-worlds-most-tech-savvy-government/283341/.

49   Ibid.

50   Dan Verton, "DHS' Identity Management Challenge Is Bigger Than You Think,"

Homeland Security Today, May 29, 2013, www.hstoday.us/columns/critical-issues-in-national-cybersecurity/blog/dhs-identity-management-challenge-is-bigger-than-you-think/fb6a2b5a2c9336376928b66f32799aa3.html.

51 Brian Robinson, "5 Tools for Improved Identity Management," *GCN*, March 9, 2015, http://gcn.com/articles/2015/03/09/id-management-tools.aspx.

52 Charles Arthur, "Gov.uk Quietly Disrupts the Problem of Online Identity Login," *The Guardian*, November 6, 2014, www.theguardian.com/technology/2014/nov/06/govuk-quietly-disrupts-the-problem-of-online-identity-login.

53 Verton, "DHS' Identity Management Challenge Is Bigger Than You Think."

54 William Jackson, "ID Management's Weakness: 'There Is No Demand,'" *GCN*, February 3, 2011, http://gcn.com/articles/2011/02/03/nstic-identity-management-challenges.aspx.

55 Gartner Inc., "The Identity Challenge Facing Digital Government," March 9, 2015, www.gartner.com/newsroom/id/3001518.

56 Bryan Glick, "GDS Targets Three Million New Users of Gov.uk Verify Service in Next 12 Months," *Computer Weekly*, July 24, 2015, www.computerweekly.com/news/4500250478/GDS-targets-three-million-new-users-of-Govuk-Verify-service-in-next-12-months.

57 Gary Simpson and Emma Lindley, "Investigating Challenges in Digital Identity: Digital Identity Inclusion and Uptake," Open Identity Exchange, 2014, p. 5, http://oixuk.org/wp-content/uploads/2014/05/Investigating-the-Challenges-in-Digital-Identity1.pdf, accessed December 8, 2015.

CHAPTER 6

1 Brian Krebs, "Was Ashley Madison Database Leaked?" *Krebs on Security*, August 15, 2015, http://krebsonsecurity.com/2015/08/was-the-ashley-madison-data-base-leaked/.

2 John Herrman, "Early Notes on the Ashley Madison Hack," *The Awl*, August 18, 2015, http://www.theawl.com/2015/08/notes-on-the-ashley-madison-hack.

3 Ibid.

4 Alastair Sharp, "Two People May Have Committed Suicide After Ashley Madison Hack: Police," *Reuters*, August 24, 2015, http://www.reuters.com/article/2015/08/24/us-ashleymadison-cybersecurity-idUSKCN0QT1O720150824.

5 Marc Goodman and Andrew Hessel, "The Bio-Crime Prophecy: DNA Hacking the Biggest Opportunity Since Cyber Attacks," *Wired*, May 28, 2013, http://www.wired.co.uk/magazine/archive/2013/06/feature-bio-crime/the-bio-crime-prophecy.

6   Michigan alone says it averages about 120,000 daily attempts, on par with the entire government of the United Kingdom. See: Brian Fung, "How Many Cyberattacks Hit the United States Last Year?" *Nextgov*, March 8, 2013, http://www.nextgov.com/cybersecurity/2013/03/how-many-cyberattacks-hit-united-states-last-year/61775/.

7   "2015 Data Breach Investigations Report," Verizon, 2015. http://www.verizon enterprise.com/DBIR/2015/.

8   Sean Lyngaas, "Exclusive: The OPM Breach Details You Haven't Seen," *FCW*, August 21, 2015, https://fcw.com/articles/2015/08/21/opm-breach-timeline.aspx.

9   Ellen Nakashima and Adam Goldman, "CIA Pulled Officers From Beijing After Breach of Federal Personnel Records," *The Washington Post*, September 29, 2015, https://www.washingtonpost.com/world/national-security/cia-pulled-officers-from-beijing-after-breach-of-federal-personnel-records/2015/09/29/1f78943c-66d1-11e5-9ef3-fde182507eac_story.html.

10   Ellen Nakashima, "Hacks of OPM Databases Compromised 22.1 Million People, Federal Authorities Say," *The Washington Post*, July 9, 2015, http://www.washingtonpost.com/blogs/federal-eye/wp/2015/07/09/hack-of-security-clearance-system-affected-21-5-million-people-federal-authorities-say/.

11   Telephone interview with John Watters, October 19, 2015.

12   Stephen Herzog, "Revisiting the Estonian Cyber Attacks: Digital Threats and Multinational Responses," *Journal of Strategic Security*, 2011, http://scholarcommons.usf.edu/cgi/viewcontent.cgi?article=105&context=jss.

13   Kertu Ruus, "Cyber War I: Estonia Attacked From Russia," European Institute, 2008, http://www.europeaninstitute.org/index.php/42-european-affairs/winterspring-2008/67-cyber-war-i-estonia-attacked-from-russia.

14   David Slade, "South Carolina: 'The Mother of All Data Breaches,'" *The Post and Courier*, November 3, 2012, http://www.postandcourier.com/article/20121103/PC16/121109713.

15   Lillian Ablon, Martin C. Libicki, and Andrea A. Golay, *Markets for Cybercrime Tools and Stolen Data: Hackers' Bazaar*, RAND Corporation, 2014, http://www.rand.org/content/dam/rand/pubs/research_reports/RR600/RR610/RAND_RR610.pdf.

16   Deloitte, *2014 Deloitte-NASCIO Cybersecurity Study: State Governments at Risk—Time to Move Forward*, October 27, 2015, p. 18, http://www2.deloitte.com/content/dam/Deloitte/us/Documents/public-sector/us-state-nascio-cybersecuritysurvey_102714.pdf.

17   Geeta Dayal, "Before Steve Jobs and Steve Wozniak Invented Apple, They Hacked Phones," *Slate*, February 1, 2013, http://www.slate.com/articles/technology/books/2013/02/steve_jobs_and_phone_hacking_exploding_the_phone_by_phil_lapsley_reviewed.2.html.

18   Marc Goodman, "Criminals Deftly Exploit the Data Deluge," May 17, 2011,
      http://www.marcgoodman.net/2011/09/15/the-economist-online-the-
      hackers-enterprise/.

19   Tom Risen, "Study: Hackers Cost More Than $445 Billion Annually," *US News
      & World Report*, June 9, 2014, http://www.usnews.com/news/articles/2014/
      06/09/study-hackers-cost-more-than-445-billion-annually.

20   Ablon, Libicki, and Golay, *Markets for Cybercrime Tools and Stolen Data*, p. 4.

21   Marc Goodman, *Future Crimes: Everything Is Connected, Everyone Is Vulnerable,
      and What We Can Do About It* (New York: Doubleday Publishing Company,
      2015), p. 185.

22   Ibid., p. 183.

23   Ablon, Libicki, and Golay, *Markets for Cybercrime Tools and Stolen Data*.

24   Goodman, "Criminals Deftly Exploit the Data Deluge."

25   Deloitte Center for Financial Services, *Transforming Cybersecurity: New
      Approaches for an Evolving Threat Landscape*, 2014, pp. 6–7,
      http://www2.deloitte.com/content/dam/Deloitte/global/Documents/
      Financial-Services/dttl-fsi-TransformingCybersecurity-2014-02.pdf.

26   SANS Institute, "CIS Critical Security Controls: Guidelines," https://www.sans
      .org/critical-security-controls/guidelines, accessed December 17, 2015.

27   Ed Powers and Mary Galligan, "The Pursuit of Cybersecurity," *Risk
      and Compliance Journal*, July 27, 2015, http://deloitte.wsj.com/
      riskandcompliance/2015/07/27/the-pursuit-of-cybersecurity/.

28   Telephone interview with Alan Paller, October 6, 2015.

29   Watters interview, October 19, 2015.

30   Vikram Mahidhar, David Schatsky, and Kelly Bissell, *Cyber Crime Fighting*,
      Deloitte University Press, June 27, 2013, http://dupress.com/articles/cyber-
      crime-fighting/.

31   Australian Signals Directorate, "ACSC—Australian Cyber Security Center,"
      http://www.asd.gov.au/infosec/acsc.htm, accessed December 17, 2015.

32   Australian Signals Directorate, "Top 4 Strategies to Mitigate Targeted Cyber
      Intrusions: Mandatory Requirement Explained," July 2013, http://www.asd
      .gov.au/infosec/top-mitigations/top-4-strategies-explained.htm.

33   Internet Storm Center, "ISC History and Overview," https://isc.sans.edu/about
      .html, accessed December 17, 2015.

34   Interview with Craig Astrich, Arlington, VA, October 9, 2015.

35   Watters interview, October 19, 2015.

36   Mohana Ravindranath, "At GSA, an 'Internet of Things' Experiment," *The
      Washington Post*, August 31, 2014, http://www.washingtonpost.com/business/
      on-it/at-gsa-an-internet-of-things-experiment/2014/08/30/403c620c-2e10-
      11e4-994d-202962a9150c_story.html.

37   Irfan Saif, Sean Peasley, & Arun Perinkolam, "Safeguarding the Internet of Things: Being Secure, Vigilant, and Resilient in the Connected Age," *Deloitte Review 17*, July 27, 2015, http://dupress.com/articles/internet-of-things-data-security-and-privacy/.

38   David A. Bray, "Democracies and Internet of Everything," *Leadership + Knowledge*, February 25, 2015, http://blog.dbray.org/2015/02/democracies-and-internet-of-everything.html?view=classic.

39   Joab Jackson, "In a Mock Cyberattack, Deloitte Teaches Business How to Respond," *Computer World*, April 8, 2015, http://www.computerworld.com/article/2907918/in-a-mock-cyberattack-deloitte-teaches-business-how-to-respond.html.

40   Sara Peters, "Cyber War Games: Top 3 Lessons Learned About Incident Response," *DarkReading*, April 7, 2015, http://www.darkreading.com/risk/cyber-war-games-top-3-lessons-learned-about-incident-response/d/d-id/1319813.

41   Deloitte, *Prepare for the Unexpected: Cyber Threat War-Gaming Can Help Decrease the Business Impact of Cyber Incidents*, 2014, http://www2.deloitte.com/content/dam/Deloitte/us/Documents/risk/us-aers-cyber-war-gaming-sales-sheet-07272014.pdf.

42   See, for instance, Deloitte, *2014 Deloitte-NASCIO Cybersecurity Study.*

43   Raytheon, *Securing Our Future: Closing the Cybersecurity Talent Gap*, October 2015, p. 2, http://www.raytheoncyber.com/rtnwcm/groups/cyber/documents/content/rtn_278208.pdf.

44   Sarah Hagen, "New USF Center Focuses on Cybersecurity," *WTSP 10 News*, February 6, 2015, http://www.wtsp.com/story/news/local/2015/02/06/sarah-hagen-10-news-cyber-security/22991529/.

45   Interview with Karen Evans, Washington, DC, August 20, 2015.

46   Anna Fifield, "Seoul Seeks Hacker Troops to Fend Off North Korean Cyberattacks," *The Washington Post,* October 25, 2015, https://www.washingtonpost.com/world/asia_pacific/south-korea-seeks-hackers-to-defend-against-north-korean-cyberattacks/2015/10/24/88bcbca0-7682-11e5-a5e2-40d6b2ad18dd_story.html.

47   Mohana Ravindranath, "No STEM Training? You Can Still Be a Defense Cyber Intel Analyst," *Nextgov*, October 30, 2015, http://www.nextgov.com/cio-briefing/wired-workplace/2015/10/officer-liberal-arts-majors-can-still-do-cyber-intel-dia/123263/?oref=ng-article-recommended.

48   Jack Moore, "Feds Say They Finally Have a Database of Every Cyber Job in Government," *Nextgov*, March 3, 2015, http://www.nextgov.com/cio-briefing/wired-workplace/2015/03/feds-say-they-finally-have-database-every-cyber-job-government/106554/.

CHAPTER 7

1   Telephone interview with Lisa Alonso Love and Greg Wells, June 1, 2015.
2   Telephone interview with Martin Stewart-Weeks, May 22, 2015.
3   Linsey Sledge and Tiffany Dovey Fishman, *Reimagining Higher Education*, Deloitte University Press, May 22, 2014, http://dupress.com/articles/reimagining-higher-education/.
4   Paul Fain, "Competency and Affordability," *Inside Higher Ed*, May 6, 2014, www.insidehighered.com/news/2014/05/06/college-america-hits-10000-mark-new-competency-based-bachelors-degrees.
5   Western Governors University, *2015 Mid-Year Report*, August 2015, http://en.calameo.com/read/002355904d6f9f949b67e.
6   Sledge and Fishman, *Reimagining Higher Education*.
7   Elizabeth D. Phillips, "Improving Advising Using Technology and Data Analytics," *Change*, January-February 2013, www.changemag.org/Archives/Back%20Issues/2013/January-February%202013/improving-advising-full.html.
8   Mark Parry, "Big Data on Campus," *The New York Times*, July 18, 2012, www.nytimes.com/2012/07/22/education/edlife/colleges-awakening-to-the-opportunities-of-data-mining.html?_r=0.
9   *ASU News*, "ASU 4-Year Graduation Rate Up 20 Points Since 2002," January 26, 2015, https://asunow.asu.edu/content/asu-4-year-graduation-rate-20-points-2002.
10 Telephone interview with Sonja Heikkilä, October 23, 2014.
11 Leon Kaye, "Helsinki Mulls a Future Free of Car Ownership," *TriplePundit*, August 6, 2014, www.triplepundit.com/2014/08/helsinki-car-ownership/.
12 Scott Corwin, Joe Vitale, Eamonn Kelly, and Elizabeth Cathles, *The Future of Mobility: How Transportation Technology and Social Trends Are Creating a New Business Ecosystem*, Deloitte University Press, September 24, 2015, http://dupress.com/articles/future-of-mobility-transportation-technology/.
13 For instance, alternative and shared modes of mobility may reduce congestion but could also lead to a decline in revenue from fuel taxes, public transportation fees, tolls, vehicle sales taxes, municipal parking, and registration and licensing fees as a result of declining individual vehicle ownership.
14 Peter Viechnicki, et al., *Smart Mobility: Reducing Congestion and Fostering Faster, Greener, and Cheaper Transportation Options*, Deloitte University Press, May 18, 2015, http://dupress.com/articles/smart-mobility-trends/.
15 Corwin, Vitale, Kelly, and Cathles, *The Future of Mobility: How Transportation Technology and Social Trends Are Creating a New Business Ecosystem*.
16 Lucas Laursen, "Barcelona's Smart City Ecosystem," *MIT Technology Review*, November 18, 2014, www.technologyreview.com/news/532511/barcelonas-smart-city-ecosystem/.

17   BCN Smart City Projects, "MobileID," http://smartcity.bcn.cat/en/
      mobileid.html, accessed on December 7, 2015.

18   Vivienne Walt, "Barcelona: The Most Wired City in the World," *Fortune*, July 29,
      2015, http://fortune.com/2015/07/29/barcelona-wired-city/.

19   Margi Murphy, "Move Over Banksy, Wallace and Gromit and Ribena; Bristol
      Will Make History as the First City to Become an Open Operating System,"
      Techworld, March 11, 2015, www.techworld.com/operating-systems/bristol-
      could-be-smartest-city-of-them-all-3601205/.

20   Motherboard, "The City That Has Its Own Operating System," October 29, 2015,
      http://motherboard.vice.com/read/the-city-that-has-its-own-operating-system.

21   Ibid.

22   SmartSantander, "Santander on FIRE (Future Internet Research &
      Experimentation)," www.smartsantander.eu/, accessed on December 7, 2015.

23   Fed4Fire, "Smart Santander," www.fed4fire.eu/smart-santander/, accessed on
      December 7, 2015.

24   Tod Newcombe, "Santander: The Smartest Smart City," *Governing*, May 2014,
      www.governing.com/topics/urban/gov-santander-spain-smart-city.html.

25   SmartSantander, "SmartSantanderRA: Santander Augmented Reality
      Application," www.smartsantander.eu/index.php/blog/item/174-
      smartsantanderra-santander-augmented-reality-application, accessed on
      December 2, 2015.

26   SIIA , "SIIA Estimates $8.38 Billion US Market for PreK–12 Educational Software
      and Digital Content," February 24, 2015, www.siia.net/Press/SIIA-Estimates-838-
      Billion-Dollars-US-Market-for-PreK-12-Educational-Software-and-Digital-Content.

27   iZone, "About the Office of Innovation," http://izonenyc.org/about-izone/.

28   Christina Quattrocchi, "New York iZone Tests Edtech Startup Efficacy,"
      edSurge, August 18, 2014, www.edsurge.com/news/2014-08-18-new-york-
      izone-tests-edtech-startup-efficacy.

29   iZone, "About the Office of Innovation: Inspiring Innovation in NYC Public
      Education."

30   US Census Bureau, "America's Economy," www.census.gov/mobile/economy/.

31   Billy Mitchell, "USDS Execs: Americans Expect Uber-Like Government,"
      FedScoop, November 12, 2015, http://fedscoop.com/usds-execs-americans-
      expect-uber-like-government.

32   James Guszcza, *The Last-Mile Problem: How Data Science and Behavioral
      Science Can Work Together*, Deloitte University Press, January 26, 2015,
      http://dupress.com/articles/behavioral-economics-predictive-analytics/.

33   Joy Forehand and Michael Greene, "Nudging New Mexico: Kindling Honesty
      Among Unemployment Claimants," *Deloitte Review 18*, http://dupress.com/
      articles/behavior-change-among-unemployment-claimants-behavioral-
      economics.

34   Philip K. Howard, *The Rule of Nobody: Saving America From Dead Laws and Broken Government* (New York: W.W. Norton & Co., 2014).

35   Don Tapscott, "Four Principles for the Open World" (talk given at TEDGlobal 2012, Edinburgh, UK, June 26, 2012).

36   John Seely Brown, "The Future of Work: Navigating the Whitewater," *Pacific Standard*, September 28, 2015, www.psmag.com/business-economics/the-future-of-work-navigating-the-whitewater.

37   Ibid.

38   Charlie Tierney, Steve Cottle, and Katie Jorgensen, *GovCloud: The Future of Government Work*, Deloitte University Press, January 1, 2012, http://dupress.com/articles/the-future-of-the-federal-workforce/?ind=74.

39   Nicole Blake Johnson, "GovConnect Makes Employee Passion Projects a Reality," *FedTech*, October 27, 2014, www.fedtechmagazine.com/article/2014/10/govconnect-makes-employee-passion-projects-reality.

40   Brad Nunnally and Sarah Allen, "Building the Next Generation Federal Workforce," 18F, September 1, 2015, https://18f.gsa.gov/2015/09/01/govconnect-launch/.

41   David S. Cohen, "Deputy Director Cohen Delivers Remarks on CIA of the Future at Cornell University," Central Intelligence Agency, September 17, 2015, https://www.cia.gov/news-information/speeches-testimony/2015-speeches-testimony/deputy-director-cohen-delivers-remarks-on-cia-of-the-future-at-cornell-university.html.

42   Dan Verton, "John Brennan's [R]evolutionary Plan for the CIA," *FedScoop*, May 4, 2015, http://fedscoop.com/john-brennans-evolutionary-plan-for-cia.

43   Cohen, "Deputy Director Cohen Delivers Remarks on CIA of the Future at Cornell University."

44   Jason Miller, "CIA Hits the Accelerator Pedal for Digital Innovation," Federal News Radio, October 7, 2015, http://federalnewsradio.com/digital-government/2015/10/cia-hits-accelerator-pedal-digital-innovation/.

45   Ibid.

46   Max Meyers, Claire Niech, and William D. Eggers, *Anticipate, Sense, and Respond: Connected Government and the Internet of Things*, Deloitte University Press, August 28, 2015, http://dupress.com/articles/internet-of-things-iot-in-government.

47   Martin Flower, "Strangler Application," Martinflower.com, June 29, 2004, www.martinfowler.com/bliki/StranglerApplication.html.

ACKNOWLEDGMENTS

While my name might be on the cover, this book was a group effort from start to finish. Dozens of talented individuals contributed to the research, writing, editing, and concept of this book.

Amrita Datar and Mahesh Kelkar of Deloitte were the book's lead researchers and contributed significantly to nearly all aspects of the book. Mahesh skillfully led the development of the chapter playbooks and contributed to numerous chapters. Amrita, a talented wordsmith, was instrumental in developing a number of case studies and contributing to many other elements of the book.

Joel Bellman, Deloitte's global lead for digital government transformation, also played a major role in the book development. He provided insightful comments on the manuscript drawing from his deep well of experience in digital. He also championed the book throughout our global network.

Two superbly talented researchers and editors, each with a deep passion for government reform, also were integral to the book's development. Dan Elbert and Jonathan Walters provided top-notch writing and editing assistance.

Bruce Wright has edited just about every book I've written—including this one—over the last decade. No one is better at sentence tightening, and I feel very fortunate to have gotten a chance to work with Bruce all these years. Jill Lawrence also did a fantastic job editing portions of the book.

Dozens of Deloitte colleagues also played critical roles. Dan Helfrich, Mark Price, Paul Macmillan, and Mike Turley provided critical leadership support for the book's development. Jonathan Copulsky and John Shumadine supported the book throughout the research process.

The design, development, and execution of the global survey that informed the book constituted a massive effort involving dozens of colleagues from dozens of Deloitte member firms from around the world. The survey analysis was led by a terrific research team with deep experience in analysis that included Pulkit Kapoor, Pankaj Kamleshkumar, and Abhijit Khuperkar of Deloitte Services LP. Becky Kapes Osmon, Sandhya Davis, and Irma Kaminska from Deloitte Touche Tohmatsu played a key role in organizing the deployment of the survey globally.

Vikrant Jain provided essential research assistance for every chapter. Matthew Budman and Aditi Rao deftly copyedited the manuscript. Steven Thai, Megan Doern, Holly Wilmot, Taylor Chronis, Sandhya Davis, and Suzanne Beck led the marketing efforts.

An advisory board of Deloitte digital transformation experts from around the world provided extensive feedback on the survey design and manuscript draft, including Art Stephens, Kristin Russell, Nathan Houser, Vance Edward Hitch, Sucha Kukatla, Greg Pellegrino, Tim Young, Jessica Kosmowski, and Rob Frazzini from Deloitte Consulting LLP in the United States; Ed Roddis from Deloitte United Kingdom; Karim Moueddene, Deloitte Belgium; Nazeer Essop, Deloitte South Africa; Paul Macmillan and Richard Carson, Deloitte Canada; Chew Chiat Lee, Deloitte Singapore; and Anindya Mallick, Deloitte India.

Numerous other Deloitte colleagues provided expert guidance on subjects ranging from cybersecurity to agile project development. Devon Halley, a friend and colleague whom I've collaborated with previously, read the full manuscript and offered some truly thoughtful feedback. Garrett Berntsen provided extensive comments on procurement reform. Paul Ballas, Rob Frazzini, Justin Franks, RJ Krawiec, Sucha Kukatla, Nelson Kunkel, Andy Main, Mark Waks, and Andy Wager of Deloitte Digital spent countless hours walking me through the fine points of digital design and delivery. Keith Cox and Nelson Wong from Deloitte Consulting LLP, as well as Jason Hutchinson of Deloitte Australia and Stephen Graham of Deloitte United Kingdom assisted with case studies in chapter 3.

Thomas Beck, Bill Beyer, Craig Logan, Akshai Prakash, David Sisk, and Van Hitch provided invaluable advice on how to make horizontal government a reality. Craig Astrich, Jason Brown, Michael Gelles, Deborah Golden, General Harry Raduege, Srini Subramanian, Matt Widmer, and Mike Wyatt took me deep into the world of cybersecurity.

Dozens of Deloitte member firms assisted with obtaining survey responses and interviewing government leaders from around the world. I'm thankful to the following individuals for their significant contributions: Sue Browne and Fran Thorn of Deloitte Australia; Wim Vergeylen and Yves Vankrunkelsven of Deloitte Belgium; Richard Carson and Jerrett Myers of Deloitte Canada; Thomas Riisom, Mark Thomasson, and Søren Brøbeck of Deloitte Denmark; Lauri Byckling and Juhana Francke of Deloitte Finland; Shane Mohan and Conor Murphy of Deloitte Ireland; Guido Borsani and Davide Iori of Deloitte Italy; Raphael Aloisio and Louisa Bartolo of Deloitte Malta; Rob Dubbeldeman, Yvonne Maas, and Hans Teuben of Deloitte Netherlands;

Dave Farrelly and John Pennington of Deloitte New Zealand; Lennart Sjøgren and Anne Cathrin Haueng of Deloitte Norway; Margarida Bajanca and Carolina Berto of Deloitte Portugal; Nazeer Essop and Gilles Stewart of Deloitte South Africa; Kim Hallenheim and Andreas Hölne of Deloitte Sweden; and Hamid Suboh and Natalia Sycheva of Deloitte UAE.

Hundreds of digital innovators were interviewed for this book. There simply isn't space to thank all of them here but I would be remiss if I didn't thank the following individuals for their time: Mike Bracken, Mike Beaven, and Kathy Settle of the UK's Government Digital Service; David Bray and Tony Summerlin from the Federal Communications Commission; Greg Godbout from the Environmental Protection Agency; Matthew Burton and Merici Vinton, formerly of the Consumer Finance Protection Bureau; Mike Bland, Hillary Hartley, Michelle Hertzfeld, Shashank Khandelwal, Eric Mill, Aaron Snow, Jennifer Tress, and Russ Unger, 18F; Conor Maguire, Alistair Montgomery, and Marc Woods of Transport for London; Kevin Cunnington and Kevin Stock from the UK Department for Work and Pensions; Jen Pahlka of Code for America; Jenn Gustetic from the Executive Office of the President, Office of Science and Technology Policy; Ger Baron from the City of Amsterdam; Jay Nath, from the City of San Francisco; Jim Wadleigh of Access Health CT; Mike Flowers of Enigma; Mike Morris of Appirio; Chris Cruz, Stuart Drown, Karen Johnson, and Kish Rajan from the State of California; Ira Rubenstein, the digital leader for PBS; Mark Naggar from the US Department of Health and Human Services; Mark Schwartz from the US Citizenship and Immigration Services (USCIS); Judy Wilson from the US Department of the Interior; Karen Evans of KE&T Partners; and Traci Walker and

Joanie Newhart, with the US Digital Service and Office of Federal Procurement Policy respectively.

Support from friends and family was incredibly important. My brother, Toph, and longtime collaborator John O'Leary provided thoughtful comments on the manuscript. Most important of all was my wife, Morgann Rose. She had to endure—for the second time in four years—watching me work countless nights and marathon weekend sessions in order to finish the book on time. Morgann could not have been more supportive throughout the process.

CONTRIBUTORS

JOEL BELLMAN

Joel Bellman is a partner in Deloitte in the United Kingdom and Deloitte's global lead for digital transformation in the public sector. He has worked extensively with central and local government organizations in the UK and elsewhere, leading programs that include building digital solutions, designing digital operating models, and delivering complex policy goals with innovative service designs. He is author of "The Ascent of Digital: Understanding and Accelerating the Public Sector's Evolution," "Making Digital Default: Understanding Citizen Attitudes," "A Mobile Enabled Government," "Red Ink Rising: Navigating the Perils of Public Debt," and "Choosing Fewer Channels: Public Service Delivery Options in an Age of Austerity." He can be reached at jbellman@deloitte.co.uk.

AMRITA DATAR

Amrita is a senior research analyst in the public sector research team. Her writing focuses on emerging trends at the intersection of technology, business, and society and how they could influence the public sector. Amrita holds bachelor's and master's degrees in economics from the University of Mumbai. She can be reached at adatar@deloitte.com.

MAHESH KELKAR

Mahesh is a research manager on Deloitte's public sector research team. His professional experience includes in-depth research and analysis in government contracting, workforce, market sizing, and analytics. Mahesh holds a bachelor's degree in industrial engineering and a masters in finance from the University of Pune. He can be reached at mkelkar@deloitte.com.

ABOUT DELOITTE UNIVERSITY PRESS

Deloitte University Press publishes original articles, reports, and periodicals that provide insights for businesses, the public sector, and NGOs. Our goal is to draw upon research and experience from throughout our professional services organization, and that of coauthors in academia and business, to advance the conversation on a broad spectrum of topics of interest to executives and government leaders.

Deloitte University Press is an imprint of Deloitte Development LLC.

ABOUT DELOITTE DIGITAL

Deloitte Digital is a digital consulting agency that brings together the creative and technology capabilities, business acumen, and industry insight needed to help transform our clients' businesses. Learn more at www.deloittedigital.com.

INDEX

ABOUT THE AUTHOR

An author, columnist, consultant, and popular speaker for more than two decades, William Eggers is a leading authority on government reform. He is the executive director of Deloitte's research center on government and higher education.

His last book, *The Solution Revolution: How Government, Business, and Social Enterprises Are Teaming Up to Solve Society's Biggest Problems* (Harvard Business Review Press 2013), which the *Wall Street Journal* calls "pulsating with new ideas about civic and business and philanthropic engagement," was named to 10 "best books of the year" lists.

His other eight books include the *Washington Post* best-seller *If We Can Put a Man on the Moon: Getting Big Things Done in Government* (Harvard Business Press, 2009), *Governing by Network* (Brookings, 2004), and *The Public Innovator's Playbook* (Deloitte Research, 2009). He also coined the term *Government 2.0* in a book by the same name.

His books have won numerous awards, including the 2014 Axiom Award for best book on business theory, the Louis Brownlow Award for best book on public management, the Sir Antony Fisher Award for best book promoting an understanding of the free economy, and the Roe Award for leadership and innovation in public policy research.

A former manager of the Texas Performance Review, he has advised governments around the world. His commentary has appeared in dozens of major media outlets including the *New York Times, Wall Street Journal,* and the *Chicago Tribune.* He lives in Washington, DC, with his wife, Morgann. He can be reached at weggers@deloitte.com or on twitter @wdeggers.